A

COMPENDIUM

OF

L N W R

LOCOMOTIVES

1912 - 1949

By Willie B. Yeadon

Part One

Passenger Tender Engines

CHALLENGER PUBLICATIONS

ISBN 1 899624 01 5

Printed and bound by Amadeus Press Ltd, Huddersfield

First published in the United Kingdom by
CHALLENGER PUBLICATIONS
15 Lovers Lane, Grasscroft, Oldham, OL4 4DP

CONTENTS

ACKNOWLEDGEMENTS

Most of those to whom I here pay tribute, sadly will not read of my grateful thanks to them, because they too have shared the fate of the LNWR. In its final years of 1919-22, I had the good fortune to find that a Mr C. Williams, at an address in Crewe, could supply an authentic printed list of names and numbers. I recall that there were two, about 16-page booklets, one in a pink, and the other in a pale blue paper cover. They helped me greatly, but about 1922/23 he produced a full list of LNWR locomotives, not only those which were named. A copy of that became my mentor and guide for the next ten years, and was then given to W.Leslie Good of Birmingham, in exchange for a goodly number of his excellent postcard size photographs to start a collection which has been steadily increased for more than sixty years now.

Fortunately, the Librarian at the National Railway Museum, Philip Atkins, was aware of the value of the data in the Williams notebooks, and secured that invaluable information for the N.R.M., where they can now be consulted in the Museum's library. Their meticulous compilation over many years of what Crewe Works did, provides a devastating riposte to those who decry railway enthusiasts as simply stupid, and they give endless pleasure to researchers.

My many years of membership in the LNWR Society has put me in contact with many who were (still are) equally concerned as myself that an accurate record, both statistical and pictorial, should be available of the locomotives which operated The Premier Line. Those members have helped me clear many obscure or debatable matters of detail, and I can best reward them by encouraging my readers to make application to join that Society.

The photographs, numbering some thousands, from which this compendium's illustrations have been selected include a considerable number which carry no reference whatever as to who took them. In more than 60 years of collecting, I find it impossible to recall sources from which I obtained them, and few indeed of the takers of LNW loco photographs now survive for me to consult. Thus I offer an omnibus acknowledgement, and if you feel that I 'have missed the bus' by not crediting any to your name, by all means tell me, through the publishers.

Tebay station as I knew it in 1913/14.

PREFACE

My dictionary defines 'compendium' as "a book containing the abstracted essentials of a larger one", and certainly this aptly fits my present work. However, the locomotives of THE PREMIER LINE were of such quantity and importance to require not just "a book", but a series of volumes. Even so, their content is limited to 'abstracted essentials', and to those locomotives which the London & North Western Railway possessed at 1912, or later added to their stock. When I made the opportunity, and time, to study LNWR locomotives, I found a surprising lack of any connected account covering them, and listing how they fared under London Midland & Scottish Railway, and under British Railways ownership. I gratefully acknowledge what Edward Talbot has published about them, but that stops at the end of 1922, and includes no complete listing. When I bought Bertram Baxter's Catalogues 2A and 2B I thought that they would provide the complete and connected stocktaking account I required. Sadly, it contains errors and omissions so I decided to try and do better, and also continue Talbot's work forward to the absolute end of what had been LNWR locomotives.
During the 35 years that I worked with the Railway Correspondence & Travel Society team of authors in the production of their 18 volumes of *Locomotives of the L.N.E.R.*, I was fully expecting that a team of LMS enthusiasts would be beavering away on researching LNWR classes to include in a parallel series of volumes. If such IS now in progress, then our experience with the LNER work, makes me believe that to do a competent job, they have left it far too late, because most of those with personal knowledge of LNWR locomotives have already shared their fate. So, at 87, I have little hope of seeing the R.C.T.S. publish any comparable account of LNWR Locomotives.
My starting point of 1912 to deal with them is chosen because that is the year they fired my enthusiasm for them, when a family holiday was spent at Shap. I can claim no 'family' tradition, or even connection, with any of this country's railways, other than very loosely. But, my uncle (by marriage) was the only one in a family of six who did *NOT* work on the LNWR, and his father was a driver at Tebay shed, at that time working his time out on the Ingleton branch. We used that in 1912 to get to Shap, and in 1913/14 to visit Tebay from our home in the West Riding. On that branch I can recall two tank engines - which I later found were Nos.1398 and 2142 - and, during the holiday visits, being taken to have tea with driver Lindsay at his home in North Terrace, the LNWR houses overlooking the station at Tebay. There, during a summer holiday you had the choice of only three activities; you could walk the fells and study sheep, you could fish in the river Lune, or you could join all the local inhabitants, and be concerned with the railway. It was an almost self-centred community, and motorcars were a real rarity in the village at that time. But the main line was a continuous source of interest, at all hours, and I will quote just one example. One August evening, at the age of six, I was allowed to stay out of bed to accompany my father, uncle, and the village postman to go down by Lune bridge to see the up Postal exchange mail bags. That was so sudden, swift, and noisy at close range that I remember nothing of it. What I do remember is that, for the first time, I was allowed to stay up to almost midnight!
Local trains apart, every train going north, express and goods alike, had to give it everything that the engine could, right from the platform end, to surmount the climb to Shap, whether it had stopped for a banking engine or not. For those coming south, the alarm bell in the station emphasized the warning to keep well back from the platform edge, and something at 75 to 80 miles per hour then whizzed before your eyes, with <u>NO</u> chance to note either engine name, or number. Just remember that in 1912 even those "magnificent men just getting into their flying machines" could do no faster than that. No wonder I became a railway enthusiast, or an LNWR fan. Tebay's thrills have only been equalled since by twice riding trains through the Canadian Rockies.

<u>NOTE REGARDING DATES USED</u>

Until August 1927, the official stock returns were based on calendar months, but the LMS accountants then changed to 4-weekly periods to provide 13 equal periods in a full year.
The dates entered in this compendium are all calendar months, so there are occasional differences between my dates and those of the accountants: but none will differ by more than a single figure. For example, their period 11/1934 covered the 4 weeks ending 3rd November, and in it, the weekly withdrawals were entered as follows:-
W.E. 13/10 - 5950/61,6001,7608,7804/18/93/5,8708/48/95 8817/56/65/6
W.E. 20/10 - 5487,6003,27563,7820/82/9,8090,8155,8794,8805/27/61/2
W.E. 27/10 - 5460,25502,25604,8260,8744/87,8813
W.E. 3/11 - 25001,25643,5930,6007
In this compendium the calendar month 10/34 is entered for all of them, whereas LMS official returns show all of them as 11/34 period.

PASSENGER TENDER ENGINES

NUMBER OF ENGINES IN EACH CLASS AT DECEMBER 31st:-

CLASS		1912	1922	1930	1939	1947	*Extinct*
2-2-2	**CORNWALL**	1	1	1	1	1	*At Museum*
2-4-0	**PRECEDENT**	124	80	18	1	1	*At Museum*
2-4-0	**WATERLOO**	53	36	10	—	—	*4/36*
4-4-0	**JUBILEE**	37	9	—	—	—	*3/25*
4-4-0	**ALFRED THE GREAT**	40	14	—	—	—	*3/28*
4-4-0	**RENOWN**	3	56	16	—	—	*12/31*
4-4-0	**PRECURSOR** Saturated	130	83	38	—	—	*9/34*
4-4-0	" Sup.& s.v.	—	7	1	—	—	*5/36*
4-4-0	" Reb.& p.v.	—	40	64	9	1	*6/49*
4-4-0	**GEORGE THE FIFTH**	60	90	90	9	3	*5/48*
4-6-0	**EXPERIMENT**	105	105	63	—	—	*9/35*
4-6-0	**PRINCE OF WALES**	40	245	246	21	6	*5/49*
4-6-0	**CLAUGHTON** as built	—	130	107	—	—	*10/35*
4-6-0	" Large boiler	—	—	20	4	1	*4/49*
	Totals	593	896	674	45	13	

The Company's armorial as displayed on the preserved engine, and a typical curved nameplate.

WEBB 2-4-0 RENEWED PRECEDENT (or LARGE JUMBO) CLASS

Officially regarded as rebuilds of the 1866 Ramsbottom and 1874 Webb designs, they were, in effect, new engines built in batches from 1887 to 1897, and then one each in 1898 and 1901, ultimately totalling 166. Withdrawals which began in December 1905, had reduced that to only 80 at the end of the LNWR on 31st December 1922. Their new owners gave those survivors LMS numbers 5000 to 5079, but 33 more were withdrawn without acquiring them, the last one being LNW 883 taken out of stock in September 1928. By the end of 1933 only No.5001 remained, and in April 1934 it was re-numbered 25001 to clear its former number for one of Stanier's standard classes. The withdrawal of 25001 in October 1934 made the Precedent class extinct.

Ramsbottom safety valves were the norm for this class, and 5018 and 25001 are believed to be the only ones changed to Ross pop type. The few other alterations made to this class concerned buffers, washout plugs, lampholders, and sanding. As built they had Webb buffers, but on most of those which survived Grouping, the LNW had replaced them with taper-shank type, which had a solid spindle. However, No.5005 still had Webb design when it took that number in June 1927, and 5012 also had them after it got that number moved to the cab side in 1928, so could have kept them until it was withdrawn in December 1930.

On most of this class there was no visible evidence of washout plugs fitted on the upper part of the firebox, but on LNW 2186 (withdrawn in December 1927), and on LMS 5029, 5031, 5039 and 5062, there were three plugs to be seen on both sides of the firebox, and they can still be seen on the preserved engine No.790 HARDWICKE. From about 1925 it was customary to change the LNW socket lampholders to LMS vertical irons, but when 5042 was ex works in April 1926, it still had sockets. Bowen Cooke began to fit his patent sandshields in 1913, to prevent sand being blown away by side winds from where it was needed, but they were being discarded before the end of the LNWR, and then only two of this class were noted so fitted. No.862 was one, and the other was No.1682, which still had them on 17th February 1923, but had them removed during the repair from which it was out as LMS 5036 in January 1924.

Fortunately a Precedent was saved to be included in the National Collection, LMS 5031 withdrawn in February 1932, being maintained in working order as 790 HARDWICKE. Although repainted to LNWR lined black, its restoration did not include reversion to Webb buffers and socket lampholders, the later taper-shank buffers, and vertical lamp irons being retained.

Change to LMS numbering was made to 47 of the class, but only the first four changed to red painting with single yellow lining, large numerals on tender, and small LMS on cab side. Those were 5012 (12/23), 5036 (1/24), 5050 (10/23), and 5069 (2/24). One more, 5039 in February 1924 got small LMS on its cab and large figures on its tender, but retained black paint. Then the cab lettering was discarded and superseded by a transfer-applied 14" circular emblem, but no more were painted red, or had number put on the tender. On 5034, 5040, 5042, 5051, 5054 and 5057, the only display of the number was a cast plate fitted on the smokebox door, and some of the tenders even kept LNWR lining. No.5057 was one which had LNW lined tender.

From January 1928, those given a repaint had the number put on the cab side, 5014 and 5048 only in 10", but 14" was standard for the others, and the tender then carried LMS lettering. 5012 still red painted, and yellow lined, had its cab lettering superseded by its number in 10" figures, and lost its smokebox plate, during a 1928 repair. After it became standard in 1928 for the engine number to be displayed on the cab, although withdrawal was proceeding at an increasing pace, at least another eleven, numbers 5000, 5001, 5002, 5005, 5011, 5018, 5029, 5031, 5045, 5062, and 5070 were so changed.

The standard tender for the class was Webb's 1800 gallon type, which had wood framing and buffer beams, axles spaced at 6' 6" and 6' 0" apart, and from 1895, carried three open coal rails. Despite Crewe following its custom of making a change of tender at each repair, this passenger class was unusual in keeping to the same type of tender throughout. 790's tender number is 375, LNW tenders having individual numbering.

919 NASMYTH built in December 1893 typifies how the class appeared until during the 1914-18 war, and shows the lining, also the LNWR crest on splasher. Note that it still has Webb buffers at both ends. In September 1926 it became 5040, and was withdrawn in August 1928.

1748 BRITANNIA at Peterborough shed on 30th September 1926 still in the unlined black painting adopted from 1917. Built in July 1889 it became 5016 in September 1927 but was withdrawn June 1928. *LCGB Ken Nunn Collection.*

1520 FRANKLIN at Bletchley, and as yet, has only had buffer change, and loss of lining. Built in May 1891, it was changed to 5027 in January 1927, then worked until withdrawn in December 1932.

RENEWED PRECEDENT CLASS AS FROM 31st DECEMBER 1912

LNW No.	NAME	Built	LMS No.	Applied	With-drawn	LNWR Cut-up No.
2190	*PRINCESS BEATRICE*	4/1875	5000	7/28	6/32	—
2191	*SNOWDON*	4/1875	5001*	3/28	10/34	—
1170	*GENERAL*	9/1878	5002	3/26	10/31	—
512	*LAZONBY*	11/1880	5003	9/26	8/29	—
256	*DUKE OF ALBANY*	1/1882	—	——	4/15	3460
271	*MINOTAUR*	6/1887	(5004)	——	12/27	—
1220	*BELTED WILL*	6/1887	—	——	3/21	3650
1485	*SMEATON*	12/1887	—	——	5/14	3483
1749	*HIBERNIA*	1/1888	—	——	5/15	3462
1522	*PITT*	1/1888	5005	6/27	6/32	—
1679	*BUNSEN*	1/1888	—	——	12/13	3506
1528	*FROBISHER*	2/1888	—	——	2/16	3459
1527	*RALEIGH*	2/1888	(5006)	——	5/25	—
379	*SEDGWICK*	10/1888	5007	3/27	2/28	—
941	*BLENKINSOP*	10/1888	(5008)	——	4/25	—
1481	*THE DUKE OF EDINBURGH*	10/1888	—	——	5/13	3486
1517	*PRINCESS HELENA*	11/1888	5009	6/26	10/28	—
1216	*PREMIER*	11/1888	—	——	3/21	3761
1480	*NEWTON*	11/1888	(5010)	——	3/28	—
696	*DIRECTOR*	11/1888	5011	9/27	12/32	—
1211	*JOHN RAMSBOTTOM*	11/1888	5012	12/23	12/30	—
1212	*PIONEER*	11/1888	5013	8/26	1/28	—
1488	*MURDOCH*	11/1888	5014	4/28	4/32	—
1685	*GLADIATOR*	11/1888	(5015)	——	11/27	—
1530	*COLUMBUS*	11/1888	—	——	11/21	3621
1748	*BRITANNIA*	7/1889	5016	9/27	6/28	—
1521	*GLADSTONE*	9/1889	(5017)	——	3/26	—
1677	*BADAJOS*	1/1890	—	——	10/22	3642
974	*RICHARD COBDEN*	1/1890	—	——	3/19	3623
1672	*TALAVERA*	2/1890	5018	3/28	12/32	—
1486	*DALTON*	3/1890	—	——	4/14	3463
1515	*MILTON*	5/1890	—	——	11/14	3516
382	*BUCKINGHAM*	5/1890	—	——	11/21	3623
308	*BOOTH*	5/1890	—	——	10/22	3638
1531	*CROMWELL*	11/1890	5019	10/27	7/28	—
1514	*SCOTT*	11/1890	—	——	1/14	3518
1214	*PRINCE ALBERT*	11/1890	—	——	4/14	3479

364 HENRY PEASE piloting ex-L&Y 10462 is leaving Oxenholme on a down Glasgow express in 1924. It became 5048 in April 1928 and was withdrawn in September 1930. Note it has a boiler with three washout plugs, but that had been changed in the later photograph as No.5048.

LNWR LOCOMOTIVES

LNW No.	NAME	Built	LMS No.	Applied	With-drawn	LNWR Cut-up No.
1674	*DELHI*	11/1890	5020	6/27	11/30	—
1484	*TELFORD*	11/1890	—	——	8/15	3496
2006	*PRINCESS*	11/1890	5021	7/26	4/32	—
396	*TENNYSON*	5/1891	—	——	11/21	3622
1673	*LUCKNOW*	5/1891	—	——	3/19	3622
1525	*ABERCROMBIE*	5/1891	5022	1/27	12/28	—
1668	*DAGMAR*	5/1891	5023	4/27	2/32	—
1675	*VIMIERA*	5/1891	(5024)	——	9/26	—
1518	*COUNTESS*	5/1891	(5025)	——	1/26	—
1519	*DUCHESS*	6/1891	5026	6/26	10/28	—
1520	*FRANKLIN*	5/1891	5027	1/27	12/32	—
380	*QUERNMORE*	6/1891	—	——	10/22	3641
1666	*ARIADNE*	6/1891	(5028)	——	9/25	—
1680	*LIVINGSTONE*	6/1891	—	——	4/13	3481
1217	*FLORENCE*	6/1891	—	——	11/15	3502
1684	*SPEKE*	6/1891	5029	12/26	9/31	—
2002	*MADGE*	6/1891	5030	8/26	12/28	—
1744	*MAGDALA*	4/1892	—	——	8/15	3491
790	*HARDWICKE*	4/1892	5031	5/28	1/32	Preserved
1213	*THE QUEEN*	4/1892	5032	3/27	2/32	—
403	*ISABELLA*	4/1892	—	——	9/22	3640
1678	*AIREY*	4/1892	(5033)	——	2/27	—
1745	*JOHN BRIGHT (GLOWWORM from 7/14)*	4/1892	5034	2/28	11/30	—
304	*HECTOR*	6/1892	5035	7/28	7/28	—
395	*SCOTIA*	6/1892	—	——	11/19	3635
1682	*NOVELTY*	6/1892	5036	1/24	7/28	—
394	*EAMONT*	4/1893	—	——	9/21	3767
942	*SHAH OF PERSIA*	4/1893	—	——	1/16	3451
381	*PATTERDALE*	4/1893	(5037)	——	12/27	—
787	*CLARENDON*	4/1893	(5038)	——	7/27	—
1667	*CORUNNA*	4/1893	5039	3/24	4/28	—
919	*NASMYTH*	12/1893	5040	9/26	8/28	—
2005	*LYNX*	1/1894	5041	6/28	12/30	—
2178	*PLUCK*	1/1894	—	——	9/22	3639
1173	*THE AUDITOR*	1/1894	5042	5/26	6/30	—
482	*PEGASUS*	1/1894	—	——	10/14	3512
2192	*CARADOC*	1/1894	(5043)	——	7/27	—
871	*PROSERPINE*	5/1894	(5044)	——	8/25	—
265	*THOMAS CARLYLE*	7/1894	5045	5/27	5/30	—
789	*BREADALBANE*	7/1894	—	——	12/14	3503
865	*ENVOY*	7/1894	5046	8/28	10/28	—
867	*DISRAELI*	7/1894	—	——	8/15	3492
256	*PRESIDENT WASHINGTON*	8/1894	(5047)	——	2/23	3649
364	*HENRY PEASE*	10/1894	5048	4/28	9/30	—
883	*PHANTOM*	8/1894	(5049)	——	9/28	—
2175	*PRECEDENT*	11/1894	—	——	4/15	3459
860	*MERRIE CARLISLE*	11/1894	5050	10/23	6/33	—
253	*PRESIDENT GARFIELD*	2/1895	—	——	8/21	3765
890	*SIR HARDMAN EARLE*	2/1895	5051	11/26	10/28	—
2182	*GIRAFFE*	2/1895	—	——	5/22	3629
749	*MERCURY*	5/1895	(5052)	——	5/27	—
945	*HUMPHREY DAVY*	6/1895	5053	4/28	12/30	—
2183	*ANTELOPE*	5/1895	5054	1/27	6/30	—
872	*WIZARD*	8/1895	—	——	5/22	3628
514	*LAWRENCE (PUCK from 6/13)*	10/1895	(5055)	——	8/26	—
260	*DUKE OF CONNAUGHT*	2/1896	—	——	8/14	3491
477	*CARACTACUS*	2/1896	(5056)	——	9/27	—
866	*COURIER*	1/1896	5057	6/26	12/28	—
517	*MARATHON*	1/1896	—	——	4/21	3762
2185	*ALMA*	1/1896	5058	2/27	11/28	—
2193	*SALOPIAN*	2/1896	(5059)	——	10/25	—
619	*MABEL*	2/1896	(5060)	——	5/26	—
1177	*PRINCESS LOUISE*	3/1896	—	——	2/20	3640
2176	*ROBERT BENSON*	4/1896	(5061)	——	6/27	—

LNW No.	NAME	Built	LMS No.	Applied	With-drawn	LNWR Cut-up No.
506	*SIR ALEXANDER COCKBURN*	7/1896	5062	6/28	2/32	—
864	*PILOT*	6/1896	(5063)	——	7/27	—
1187	*CHANDOS*	7/1896	5064	3/27	9/30	—
1193	*JOSHUA RADCLIFFE*	8/1896	—	——	3/13	3460
478	*COMMODORE*	8/1896	(5065)	——	9/26	—
2194	*CAMBRIAN*	10/1896	(5066)	——	5/25	—
2186	*LOWTHER*	1/1896	(5067)	——	12/27	—
869	*LLEWELLYN*	11/1896	—	——	1/22	3625
1194	*MIRANDA*	2/1897	5068	2/28	6/30	—
2187	*PENRITH BEACON*	12/1896	5069	2/24	6/32	—
262	*WHEATSTONE*	4/1897	5070	2/28	6/32	—
480	*DUCHESS OF LANCASTER*	2/1897	(5071)	——	9/27	—
193	*ROCKET*	3/1897	(5072)	——	1/26	—
2180	*PERSEVERANCE*	3/1897	(5073)	——	2/26	—
2184	*REYNARD*	5/1897	—	——	3/19	3625
2179	*PATIENCE*	5/1897	—	——	3/20	3643
1189	*STEWART*	6/1897	—	——	12/22	3634
857	*PRINCE LEOPOLD*	7/1897	(5074)	——	7/28	—
862	*BALMORAL*	7/1897	5075	9/28	8/31	—
2189	*AVON*	7/1897	(5076)	——	8/27	—
1105	*HERCULES*	12/1897	(5077)	——	7/28	—
870	*FAIRBAIRN*	3/1898	5078	9/28	12/28	—
861	*AMAZON*	9/1901	(5079)	——	8/25	—

It will be noticed that the cut-up numbers applied by Crewe Works are duplicated in a few cases. It was a common LNW practice to recycle cut-up numbers.

** 5001 changed to 25001 in 4/34.*

1187 CHANDOS built in July 1896 is here at Nottingham on 28th September 1926, and apart from being unlined, is still in original condition. Changed to 5064 in March 1927, it was withdrawn in September 1930. *LCGB Ken Nunn Collection.*

(below) **1675 VIMIERA at Keswick on June 17th 1919 has the 11.20 ex Cockermouth which it worked on to Penrith. It has not been altered and is lined. Built May 1891, it was allotted LMS 5024 but did not carry it, being withdrawn in September 1926.** *LCGB Ken Nunn Collection.*

193 ROCKET on 2nd August 1920 in Carlisle on an up express, still has no alterations and is lined. Built May 1897 it was intended to be LMS 5072 but was withdrawn in January 1926 without being re-numbered. Note tender is unlined. *LCGB Ken Nunn Coll.*

862 BALMORAL is in plain black, has had buffer change, and been fitted with sandshields, but those were removed before the end of the LNWR. *Rail Archive Stephenson.*

1488 MURDOCH is piloting a Claughton (and letting it do all the work) on an up express at Wreay in 1924. It has changed to taper-shank buffers and is in unlined black. Built in November 1888, it changed in April 1928 to LMS 5014 and was withdrawn in April 1932. *L&GRP.*

(above) **5018 TALAVERA took that number in March 1928 when it got this final livery. To the buffer change, it now has lamp irons, and Ross pop safety valves. Its LNW no.8 (Rugby) shed plate has been moved to the smokebox door from the rear edge of the cab roof, showing photograph to be in 1931 or 32.**

(right) **5029 SPEKE, here at Crewe station, took that number in December 1926 and had it moved to cab after January 1928. It has a boiler with its washout plugs visible, and this shows their position on the driving side. It had been built in June 1891, and was withdrawn in Sept.1931.**

5062 SIR ALEXANDER COCKBURN only got that number in June 1928, but this right hand view shows the plug positions were deliberately not opposite. Curiously it had been LNW 506: it was withdrawn February 1932. *LPC.*

5005 PITT changed to that number in June 1927, when emblem was put on cab and number on a tender which actually kept LNW lining. Note that it still had Webb buffers and socket lampholders, here at Manchester (London Road) station having worked in from Altrincham.

5005 with number moved to cab is at Chester shed in 1931 and has had significant changes. It has boiler showing plugs, taper-shank buffers, lamp sockets replaced by irons, and shed plate on door. Withdrawal was in July 1932. Photographed 1931/32.

2185 ALMA built in January 1896 shows the appearance of many of the class when handed over by the LNWR to the LMS. In 1917, war conditions stopped lining being applied, but that was able to be resumed during 1921 and here the cab carries it in two panels. None however seem to have recovered the armorial on the splasher. 2185 changed to 5058 in February 1927 but then only survived until November 1928.

5000 PRINCESS BEATRICE probably took that initial LMS number due either to ignorance, or false pretence, based on a building date of April 1875. Four of the original Webb Precedents were not "renewed" but simply regarded as "rebuilt" because they then kept their 7/8" frames. 2190 was "rebuilt" in November 1895, which would have put it around 5056. Instead it got 5000 applied in July 1928 and was withdrawn July 1932. The engine is seen stored at Rugby. *Real Photos.*

5036 was one of only four given the full LMS painting which Crewe applied briefly from October 1923 to February 1924. As 1682 NOVELTY (an appropriate name) it changed to 5036 in January 1924 on red paint with yellow lining and LMS initials, which it kept to withdrawal in July 1928.

5039 CORUNNA had changed from LNW 1667 in March 1924, but complete re-organisation of Crewe Works halted painting, so whilst it got LMS on the cab and number on the tender, it kept unlined black paint, as here on September 30th 1926 at Peterborough shed, and to its April 1928 withdrawal. *LCGB Ken Nunn Collection.*

5054 ANTELOPE was re-numbered from LNW 2183 in January 1927 whilst the circular emblem was being put on cab sides. Its tender remained plain black and anonymous, but the engine was another which had only the cast plate at the front, and so remained until withdrawal in June 1930. *R.K.Blencowe Collection.*

5019 CROMWELL changed from LNW 1531 in October 1927, and although it had tender number, on the engine, the 1531 plates were simply removed from the cab sides and superseded by one cast plate on the smokebox door. This indignity only lasted 9 months because it was withdrawn in July 1928. *Real Photos.*

5048 HENRY PEASE from April 1928 had been LNW 364, and from January 1928 number on cab was made standard, with LMS on tender in 14" lettering. 5048 (also 5014) both done in April 1928 only had numbers 10" high on cab; 5048 was withdrawn in September 1930.

5070 WHEATSTONE had number put on cab in February 1928, changing from LNW 262. It and all others with cab number (except 5012) got 14 inch figures, but 5070's tender did not have LMS put on for some reason.

25001 was so altered in April 1934 to clear its 5001 number for use by one of Stanier's standard classes, but when withdrawn in October 1934, only the preserved "Hardwicke" was left of the class. Note rare use of pop type safety valves. *Real Photos.*

1682 NOVELTY could have been the last one with sandshields on, as seen here at Crewe on 17th February 1923. Note that it then still had Webb buffers fitted, and there was no lining on the engine or tender.

5034 GLOWWORM changed to that number in February 1928, and only carried it on a cast plate fitted to the smokebox door, the cab panel being left blank although later 5034 was added, but only in 10" figures. Here it is at Carlisle. *N.E.Preedy Collection.*

5012 JOHN RAMSBOTTOM in December 1923 was one of the four to get red painting, having changed from LNW 1211, and also to taper-shank buffers. Here in 1924 at Carlisle, as pilot to exL&Y 1670, it awaits arrival of an express from Scotland, to take it on over Shap summit.

5012's red livery survived its change of number position to cab side in 1928, for which only 10" figures were used. It was also exceptional by having reversion to Webb buffers, which it then kept to December 1930 withdrawal. This is Rugby shed yard in 1928. *W.L.Good 2137.*

5051 SIR HARDMAN EARLE had been LNW 890 until re-numbered in November 1926, when it acquired smokebox plate and circular emblem on cab, but appears to have plain tender. This would be its final guise as it was withdrawn in October 1928.

5050 MERRIE CARISLE is in red livery, one of only four so painted. Even the end of the buffer beam got a lining panel.

790 HARDWICKE was a static exhibit in Clapham Museum, but when in 1975 it moved to the National Railway Museum at York, its running condition was restored. Here on 24th April 1976 at Poppleton, it is on a fan trip from Gainsborough to Carnforth. Note its boiler is one with the washout plugs visible. *T.J.Edgington.*

WEBB 2-4-0 "WATERLOO" (or SMALL JUMBO) CLASS

This was also known as the "Whitworth" class, the engine of that name being the first into traffic, although the one named Waterloo had an earlier works number. They were very similar to the Precedent class, differing only by having 6" smaller coupled wheels, and were regarded as replacement rebuilds of Ramsbottom's "Samson" class of 1863, although they were really new engines. Ninety were added to stock from September 1889 to November 1896, but scrapping had reduced that to only 36 by the end of the LNWR. Two more were withdrawn in January 1923, and another four were transferred to Departmental Stock for the use of District Engineers, which left 30 for the LMS to allocate numbers 5080 to 5109. Further withdrawals, to that of No.934 NORTH STAR in January 1928, resulted in only fourteen taking up LMS numbers, and when 5095 was withdrawn in March 1932, it was the last in Capital Stock, but the class did not become extinct until April 1936 when ENGINEER WATFORD was scrapped.

Most of those which became LMS owned had a boiler on which no evidence of plugs for washing out was visible, but on 5084, 5087 and ENGINEER WATFORD, three plugs could be seen. Safety valves of Ramsbottom type were retained by most of the class, but in the 1930's, both ENGINEER LANCASTER and ENGINEER WATFORD changed to Ross pop type.

By Grouping, most of their original Webb buffers had been replaced by the taper shank type with solid spindle, but No.5092 VIOLET still had Webb buffers when it was withdrawn in April 1930. There was also a change from sockets to irons for the lamps on engines shopped from 1925, although sockets remained on 5088 until it was withdrawn in December 1928. Only ENGINEER MANCHESTER has been noted with sandshields fitted, and they were probably removed before the end of the LNWR.

None of this class acquired red painting, but 5092 and ENGINEER LIVERPOOL did get the LMS circular emblem on their splashers. When numbers were put on cabs, 5083, 5084, 5088 and 5104 got 10", and 5087 with 5092 got 14" figures, to which 5104 changed later, all having large LMS on the tender. 5102 also had 14" number but its tender was plain black. The Departmental engines were bereft of any numbering, but had an LNW style cast plate on cab panel showing their allocation. As they did a lot of running tender-first, a spectacle plate, or a meagre cab, was fitted at the front of their tender. All tenders coupled with this class were Webb 1800 gallon type, which had wood framing and buffer beam, unequal axle spacing, and three open coal rails.

1045 WHITWORTH was the first into traffic, in September 1889, and although allocated LMS 5081 it remained as seen here until withdrawn in February 1926. It still just has lined livery but has had front buffers changed to taper shank type.

5088 CHARON was LNW 735 until October 1926 and also retained sockets until its December 1928 withdrawal, but had changed its buffer type. Its boiler shows no sign of washout plugs to the top of the firebox.

(above) **742 SPITFIRE lost number and name in July 1921 when transferred to Departmental Stock as ENGINEER LIVERPOOL (see photo page 16). During a 1924 repair it acquired the LMS circular emblem on its splashers, but on black paint as seen here at Edge Hill, and then retained it to October 1932 withdrawal. No.5092 also got the emblem when renumbered in August 1927.**

5083 HENRIETTA was LNW 814 until May 1928 when its new number was put on cab side. It got only 10" figures, and was fortunate to be photographed as such because it was withdrawn only two months later, in July 1928. *R.Blencowe Collection.*

5104 WOODLARK first had its LMS number in 10" figures which would date from March 1927, and it then still had socket lampholders.

901 HERO is seen leaving Crewe for the north in 1922 as pilot to an L&Y 4-4-2 being tried on the West Coast Main Line. It still has Webb buffers and lamp sockets, and in March 1927 was renumbered to LMS 5085.

5104 WOODLARK renumbered from LNW 784 in March 1927, here has the standard 14" figures, and would be as seen here when it was withdrawn in October 1931, when only 5084/95 then remained.

5092 VIOLET took that number in August 1927 from LNW 763, but when withdrawn in April 1930, it still had Webb buffers and lamp sockets.

ENGINEER LIVERPOOL had been 742 SPITFIRE until July 1921 when this lined livery was restored, and tender cab was fitted in connection with its use as a Departmental Locomotive.

(*above*) 5102 was one of the few Small Jumbos to get 14" cab numbering, having had that number from February 1926, and here working a passenger stopping train at St.Bees, it has a plain tender. Note that it was one to change from sockets to lamp irons.

Here in Crewe Works paint shop, ENGINEER CREWE has been replated in January 1932 to ENGINEER SOUTH WALES, and was then transferred there until it was withdrawn in August 1933.
C.L.Turner.

(above) **ENGINEER CREWE was LNW 209 PETREL until July 1914 when transferred to Departmental Stock. Here in LMS years its tender has only a spectacle plate fitted. Note the brackets on the tender for the communication cord.**
Real Photos.

(right) **ENGINEER CREWE, on South shed 29th November 1931, with a mini-cab instead of just a spectacle plate, and different arrangement of spectacle windows and of the communication cord. In the following January it moved to be ENGINEER SOUTH WALES, and was withdrawn in August 1933.**

ENGINEER WATFORD from May 1923, this engine had been 793 MARTIN, and was to have been LMS 5101 but went into Departmental Stock. Note its boiler is one with three washout plugs, and also has Ross pop safety valves. When withdrawn in April 1936 it was the last of the class.

(right) **792 THEOREM had been intended to take LMS 5099 but in late 1923 it became Departmental Locomotive ENGINEER - seen here at Crewe South on 7th June 1931. It was withdrawn on July 1932, and had retained Webb buffers.** *A.B.Crompton.*

(below) **ENGINEER LANCASTER was in Departmental stock from February 1924 until its withdrawal in June 1935. Previously it was 737 ROBERTS and would have taken LMS 5100 if it had remained in Capital Stock.** *C.A.J.Nevett.*

ENGINEER LANCASTER working his saloon over Brock water troughs.

WATERLOO (or WHITWORTH) CLASS as from 31st December 1912

LNW No.	NAME	Built	LMS No.	Applied	Withdrawn	Cut-up No.
748	*WATERLOO*	11/1889	5080	3/24	4/25	—
1045	*WHITWORTH*	9/1889	(5081)	—	2/26	—
731	*CROXTETH*	11/1889	—	—	1/23	3646
733	*CHIMERA*	1/1890	(5082)	—	9/26	—
814	*HENRIETTA*	1/1890	5083	5/28	7/28	—
758	*HARDMAN*	1/1890	—	—	8/22	3656
231	*FIREFLY*	6/1890	—	—	8/22	3637
642	*BEE*	8/1890	5084	3/28	1/32	—
901	*HERO*	10/1890	5085	3/27	12/28	—
36	*THALABA*	10/1890	—	—	7/22	3632
468	*WILDFIRE*	10/1890	(5086) ENGINEER NORTHAMPTON 5/23 to 12/27			
604	*NARCISSUS*	11/1890	5087	10/26	9/30	—
736	*MEMNON*	1/1892	—	—	2/15	3454
735	*CHARON*	1/1892	5088	10/26	12/28	—
633	*SAMSON*	1/1892	—	—	1/13	3433
934	*NORTH STAR*	3/1892	(5089)	—	1/28	—
752	*GLOWWORM*	3/1892	—	—	2/13	3451
479	*MASTODON*	3/1892	—	—	12/13	3502
124	*MARQUIS DUORO*	3/1893	5090	5/28	10/28	—
634	*ELLESMERE*	3/1893	5091	5/28	7/28	—
485	*EUXINE*	3/1893	to 3760 in 3/21 and ENGINEER SOUTH WALES to 1/32			
763	*VIOLET*	3/1893	5092	8/27	4/30	—
764	*SHAP*	3/1893	(5093)	-	2/26	—
742	*SPITFIRE*	3/1893	to 3766 in 3/21 and ENGINEER LIVERPOOL to 10/32			
609	*THE EARL OF CHESTER*	4/1893	(5094) ENGINEER WALSALL from 6/23 to 2/28			
739	*SUTHERLAND* (*OSTRICH from 6/13*)	4/1893	—	—	1/23	3645
446	*SIREN*	4/1893	—	—	6/15	3479
628	*TARTARUS*	4/1893	5095	4/26	3/32	—
817	*CONSTANCE*	4/1893	(5096)	—	6/27	—
824	*ADELAIDE*	6/1893	5097	7/26	4/29	—
2153	*ISIS*	6/1893	—	—	11/14	3505
795	*FALSTAFF*	6/1893	—	—	3/14	3462
486	*SKIDDAW*	6/1893	(5098)	—	12/27	—
792	*THEOREM*	6/1893	(5099) to ENGINEER from 5/23 to 4/32			
737	*ROBERTS*	5/1894	(5100) ENGINEER LANCASTER from 2/24 to 6/35			
404	*ZOPHYRUS*	3/1894	—	—	4/13	3483
2154	*LOADSTONE*	3/1894	—	—	2/13	3452
793	*MARTIN*	5/1894	(5101) ENGINEER WATFORD from 5/23 to 4/36			
2152	*SYBIL*	5/1894	—	—	2/14	3451
90	*LUCK OF EDENHALL*	5/1894	—	—	9/15	3489
401	*ZENO*	5/1894	—	—	6/15	3483
1168	*CUCKOO*	6/1894	5102	2/26	7/31	—
732	*HECLA*	1/1895	(5103)	—	9/27	—
794	*WOODLARK*	1/1895	5104	3/27	10/31	—
2158	*SISTER DORA*	1/1895	(5105)	—	9/27	—
2156	*SPHINX*	2/1895	to 3488 then ENGINEER MANCHESTER 6/14 to 10/27			
209	*PETREL*	8/1895	to 3496 then ENGINEER CREWE 7/14 to 5/32 ENGINEER SOUTH WALES 5/32 to 8/33			
487	*JOHN O'GROAT*	8/1895	—	—	8/19	3631
773	*CENTAUR*	7/1895	(5106)	—	12/24	—
424	*SIRIUS*	7/1895	(5107)	—	9/27	—
885	*VAMPIRE*	1/1896	—	—	3/16	3458
1166	*WYRE*	1/1896	5108	3/24	12/27	—
2157	*UNICORN*	11/1896	(5109)	—	7/25	—

WEBB 4-4-0 FOUR-CYLINDER COMPOUND "JUBILEE" CLASS

Starting in June 1897 with two examples, 1501 as a 4-cylinder simple, and 1502 as a 4-cylinder compound, Webb decided, after just over a year, on the compound and another 38 were built from March 1899 to October 1900, taking numbers 1903 to 1940. In May 1898 the first engine was changed from simple to compound working, and in March 1899, 1501 and 1502 became 1901 and 1902 to take their place at the head of the production batch. Originally named IRON DUKE, in December 1897, No.1501 was changed to JUBILEE, and the plate also had a red diamond at each end of the name.

When Whale succeeded Webb, he duly simplified this class, and in June 1908 rebuilt No.1918 RENOWN as an uncomplicated 4-4-0 using the two existing cylinders between the frames, resulting in some very useful engines for secondary passenger trains. Two more were changed similarly by Cooke in March 1910, and the process had begun to gather momentum when the 1914 war slowed it down considerably. At its end in November 1918, only eleven "Jubilees" had been changed to "Renowns", but by the demise of the LNWR on 31st December 1922, only nine Jubilees remained. In 1923/24, the LMS rebuilt six of them and scrapped the other three, the withdrawal of No.1923 in March 1925 marking the end of the Jubilee class compounds.

In 1904, two boilers for the Jubilee class were built with Belpaire firebox, and put into Nos.1929 and 1930. When the latter was changed to a Renown in April 1916, its Belpaire firebox boiler became spare, but then found further use on No.1912 from 1921 until February 1924, when that engine was changed to a Renown. Use of this square-top firebox involved cab windows being changed from circular to shaped.

It was on this class that Webb introduced the large circular boss for the coupled wheel centres, a feature which both Whale and Cooke worked into their designs. When new the "Jubilees" had plain top to their chimney, but Whale added quite a deep capuchon to most of them, but it is doubtful if No.1904 was ever so fitted. The normal safety valves were of Ramsbottom type, but the last one to be in this class, No.1911 latterly had been fitted with Ross pop type on a Ramsbottom mounting.

As "Jubilee" class, all retained socket lamp holders, but where replacement of buffers was needed, the original Webb parallel shank with hollow spindle type was changed to those with taper shank and solid spindle, all having steel plate buffer beam.

The nine at Grouping became eight by No.1923's withdrawal in January 1923, and the LMS allocated the numbers 5110 to 5117 to them, but none of these were applied whilst still compounds. All had and kept the Webb tender with wooden frames and the three open coal rails.

WEBB'S JUBILEE CLASS as 4-CYLINDER COMPOUNDS

LNW No.	NAME	Built	To 2-Cyl. Simple	Renown Class or Withdrawn
1901	*IRON DUKE (JUBILEE from 12/97)*	6/1897	4/19	—
1902	*BLACK PRINCE*	6/1897	8/19	—
1903	*IRON DUKE*	3/1899	5/24	—
1904	*ROB ROY*	3/1899	—	5/23 as 3622
1905	*BLACK DIAMOND*	3/1899	8/14	—
1906	*ROBIN HOOD*	4/1899	5/17	—
1907	*BLACK WATCH*	4/1899	2/22	—
1908	*ROYAL GEORGE*	4/1899	—	1/23 as 3648
1909	*CRUSADER*	4/1899	11/19	—
1910	*CAVALIER*	4/1899	8/21	—
1911	*CENTURION*	6/1899	12/24	—
1912	*COLOSSUS*	6/1899	5/24	—
1913	*CANOPUS*	6/1899	3/10	—
1914	*INVINCIBLE (re-no. 1257 in 4/20)*	6/1899	9/16	—
1915	*IMPLACABLE*	6/1899	11/23	—
1916	*IRRESISTIBLE*	7/1899	2/19	—
1917	*INFLEXIBLE*	7/1899	8/22	—
1918	*RENOWN*	7/1899	6/08	—
1919	*RESOLUTION*	8/1899	11/19	—
1920	*FLYING FOX*	8/1899	12/20	—
1921	*T.H.ISMAY (JOHN O'GAUNT from 4/13)*	2/1900	4/13	—
1922	*INTREPID*	2/1900	10/16	—
1923	*AGAMEMNON*	3/1900	—	3/25
1924	*POWERFUL*	3/1900	6/22	—
1925	*WARRIOR*	3/1900	4/17	—
1926	*LA FRANCE*	3/1900	3/22	—
1927	*GOLIATH*	3/1900	1/24	—
1928	*GLATTON*	4/1900	8/21	—
1929	*POLYPHEMUS*	4/1900	2/24	—
1930	*RAMILLIES*	4/1900	4/16	—
1931	*AGINCOURT*	9/1900	12/21	—
1932	*ANSON*	9/1900	6/20	—
1933	*BARFLEUR*	9/1900	4/21	—
1934	*BLENHEIM*	9/1900	9/20	—
1935	*COLLINGWOOD*	10/1900	3/10	—
1936	*ROYAL SOVEREIGN*	10/1900	6/17	—
1937	*SUPERB*	10/1900	1/19	—
1938	*SULTAN*	10/1900	2/20	—
1939	*TEMERAIRE*	10/1900	8/19	—
1940	*TRAFALGAR*	10/1900	4/21	—

(opposite top) **1501 IRON DUKE built June 1897 was a 4-cylinder simple to compare with Webb's first 4-cylinder compound passenger engine No.1502. As early as March 1899 it was rebuilt to compound working, having been re-named Jubilee, and re-numbered 1901. It was again rebuilt in April 1919 as a Renown.** *LPC.*

(opposite bottom) **1918 RENOWN was one of the 38 Jubilee compounds built from March 1899 to October 1900, and here is at Bletchley in 1902. It has all original features - Ramsbottom safety valves, no plugs visible, plain chimney top, lubricator on side of smokebox, Webb buffers, socket lampholders, and 2000 gallon tender with three open coal rails, and unequal axle spacing.** *A.G.Ellis Collection.*

1502 built June 1897 as a compound, changed to 1902 in March 1899 but kept its name. From new, its double chimney and blastpipes aimed at equalising the draught through the tubes, but were soon removed. In April 1919 it was rebuilt to Renown class. *Real Photos.*

1902 BLACK PRINCE renumbered from 1502, with chimney changed to single blast pipe type, and now with full lining on its black paint, as running from March 1899. *LNWR Soc.*

1904 ROB ROY remained Jubilee class until withdrawn in May 1923, and probably kept chimney without capuchon, because this is a post-1917 photo showing unlined black, and it is fitted with Cooke buffers and his patent sandshields.

RENOWN was the first to be rebuilt (in June 1908) to 2-cylinder simple, and here in Broad Street on 1st February 1910 has the inaugural 5.25 p.m. to Birmingham. All Jubilees except 1904/8/23 were changed similarly, 1911 rebuilt December 1924 being last of the class.

1929 POLYPHEMUS, at Crewe North, got one of the two boilers with Belpaire firebox built in 1904 for this class, and kept it until it became a Renown in February 1924. Note buffer change, lubricator on smokebox removed, and fitting of capuchon to chimney, also Cooke sandshields. *Real Photos.*

1917 INFLEXIBLE at Llandudno in 1915 shows the deep capuchon on the chimney, also the fitting of sandshields. The original lamp sockets, and Webb buffers are clearly seen, as are the Ramsbottom safety valves. It has lined livery and remained a Jubilee to August 1922. *A.G.Ellis Collection.*

1911 CENTURION was the only Jubilee class to be changed to Ross pop safety valves, probably post-war because it is in unlined black, and when rebuilt to Renown in December 1924 it was last of the class. *Real Photos.*

1912 COLOSSUS is on the North Wales coast line, and leaving the station at Colwyn Bay on an up express about 1919, because it is in the wartime black without lining. Still on express work, this is probably a Llandudno to Manchester (Exchange) train.

1914 carried the name INVINCIBLE from new, through its September 1916 rebuilding to Renown class, but the number was changed to 1257 in April 1920 to release 1914 for the Company's War Memorial engine to take it. *Lens of Sutton.*

ALFRED THE GREAT CLASS - As built, and as altered 1903-07 to BENBOW CLASS

From May 1901 to August 1903, Crewe built another forty numbers 1941-80 differing only from the Jubilee class by having 4" larger diameter boiler. Their valve gear was the same arrangement, whereby that for the low pressure inside cylinders worked the valves of the high pressure outside cylinders by rocking levers, and was not independently variable which, on the 3-cylinder compounds had proved an advantage. In March 1903, just before his retirement, Webb signed drawings for the outside cylinders to have separately adjustable Joy valve gear, and for it, a larger casing on the running plate was needed. Before any were altered Whale had taken over, and in July 1903, he signed drawings for a rearward extension of the cab roof with support for it by extending the vertical handrails.

Ex works in September 1903 No.1952 BENBOW had undergone both modifications, and all the other 39 had been altered similarly by the end of 1907, the class then being known as Benbows. Curiously, the separation of valve gear adjustment, and cab roof extension, was never applied to the Jubilee class. When Whale got around to dealing with them, the rebuilding of RENOWN in March 1908 showed his idea of how to improve that class. It proved so effective that, from April 1913, Cooke began to convert the Benbows to Renowns, and by the end of the LNWR, 25 had been so changed. In 1923/24 another eight were converted, the remaining seven being scrapped from December 1922, still as Benbow compounds. No.1948 in February 1927 was the last of those normal Benbows, but in May 1921, Beames had a superheater put into No.1974 and that one still worked as a compound until its withdrawal in March 1928 cleared the Benbow class.

Most, but not all, acquired a capuchon on their chimney, even before their conversion to Benbows, and when buffer replacements were needed, taper shank type was fitted in place of the Webb type. Unlike the Jubilees, no Benbow seems to have changed to Ross pop safety valves, or to Belpaire firebox, and in that class they retained socket lamp holders. Only the superheated 1974 got a mechanical lubricator.

Due to 1976 being scrapped in December 1922, and 1956 in February 1923, it left thirteen to be allocated LMS nos. 5118 - 5130 but none were applied whilst they were still in Benbow class.

1950 VICTORIOUS, leaving Manchester (London Road), was one of the forty, nos. 1941 - 1980 built May 1901 to August 1903 similar to the Jubilee class but with boiler 4" bigger in diameter, although the valve gear was the same and not independently variable for the h.p. and l.p. cylinders. Webb knew that was a drawback, and before he retired had drawings produced for alteration to Joy valve gear, but none had been changed.

1975 JUPITER shows the alterations made by Whale, the casing ahead of the splasher being needed to house the Joy gear for the outside cylinder. Whale also had the cab roof extended and supported by pillars. The first done, in September 1903 was 1952 BENBOW and all were done by December 1907. 1975 is outside Manchester (London Road).

ALFRED THE GREAT CLASS 4-CYLINDER COMPOUNDS

LNW No.	NAME	Built	To 2 cyl Simple	Renown Class or Withdrawn
1941	*ALFRED THE GREAT*	5/1901	2/22	—
1942	*KING EDWARD VII*	5/1901	9/22	—
1943	*QUEEN ALEXANDRA*	6/1901	9/16	—
1944	*VICTORIA AND ALBERT*	6/1901	—	2/27
1945	*MAGNIFICENT*	6/1901	9/15	—
1946	*DIADEM*	6/1901	10/14	—
1947	*AUSTRALIA (ZILLAH from 6/11)*	6/1901	9/21	—
1948	*CAMPERDOWN*	6/1901	10/15	—
1949	*KING ARTHUR*	6/1901	1/18	—
1950	*VICTORIOUS*	6/1901	10/22	—
1951	*BACCHANTE*	1/1902	10/13	—
1952	*BENBOW*	1/1902	11/23	—
1953	*FORMIDABLE*	2/1902	12/23	—
1954	*GALATEA*	2/1902	10/24	—
1955	*HANNIBAL*	2/1902	—	8/23 as 3630
1956	*ILLUSTRIOUS*	2/1902	—	1/23 as 3647
1957	*ORION*	3/1902	4/17	—
1958	*ROYAL OAK*	3/1902	4/22	—
1959	*REVENGE*	3/1902	4/16	—
1960	*FRANCIS STEVENSON*	3/1902	2/18	—
1961	*ALBEMARLE*	2/1903	9/15	—
1962	*AURORA*	2/1903	6/21	—
1963	*BOADICEA*	2/1903	6/20	—
1964	*CAESAR*	2/1903	9/24	—
1965	*CHARLES H.MASON*	2/1903	8/17	—
1966	*COMMONWEALTH*	2/1903	—	4/25
1967	*CRESSY*	3/1903	11/23	—
1968	*CUMBERLAND*	3/1903	6/20	—
1969	*DOMINION*	3/1903	4/24	—
1970	*GOOD HOPE*	3/1903	4/24	—
1971	*EURYALUS*	7/1903	4/13	—
1972	*HINDUSTAN*	7/1903	3/21	—
1973	*HOOD*	7/1903	9/21	—
1974	*HOWE*	7/1903	—	3/28
1975	*JUPITER*	7/1903	1/21	—
1976	*LADY GODIVA*	7/1903	—	12/22 as 3644
1977	*MARS*	7/1903	2/24	—
1978	*MERLIN*	7/1903	12/21	—
1979	*NELSON*	7/1903	—	8/23 as 3631
1980	*NEPTUNE*	8/1903	5/22	—

1972 HINDOSTAN rebuilt to Benbow class shows two small details introduced by Whale, and differing from 1941-80 as built. Note capuchon added to chimney, and removal of the cylindrical lubricator for the inside cylinders on the smokebox side. 1972 stands on the engine servicing road at Manchester (London Road). It was rebuilt to Renown class in March 1921.

1974 HOWE was the only one of the forty to be superheated and to have mechanical lubricator fitted. Beames made that alteration to it in May 1921, and it still ran as a compound to withdrawal in March 1928, and in LNWR lined livery; then Benbows were extinct.

1942 KING EDWARD VII has probably been paired with this tender for official photograph to be taken. It is one of Whale's design which began the change from wood to steel framing. 1941-50 had Webb 2000 gallon type with unequal axle spacing, whilst 1951-80 got 2500 gallon type with equally spaced axles, both having three open coal rails. Few Benbows actually ran with a Whale tender, but 1944 VICTORIA AND ALBERT was doing so when seen at Northampton on 7th August 1920. *Railway Photographs.*

1947 AUSTRALIA has a Webb 2000 gallon tender here, and whilst capuchon has been added, it still has lubricator on smokebox side. In June 1911 its name changed to ZILLAH, and it was rebuilt to a Renown in September 1921. Here it is at Stockport in 1909.

1977 MARS at Willesden shed on 3rd June 1922 with Webb 2500 gallon tender, which had axles equally spaced, and as first fitted to 1951-80. Note that it is in the plain black painting which had to be used from 1917 due to wartime labour shortage. Note Cooke sandshields have been fitted.
N.E.Preedy Coll.

WHALE "RENOWN" CLASS 2-CYLINDER SIMPLE REBUILDS

Having disposed of problems with compounds on the main line expresses, by putting 130 new Precursor class in place of the temperamental Webb 3-cylinder compounds, Whale then turned his attention to the 4-cylinder compounds. From the Jubilee class he was able to make a smaller version of his reliable Precursors. The prototype, which gave the class its name, was No.1918 RENOWN, rebuilt in June 1908. It used the same type boiler as the Alfred the Great class, and the existing inside cylinders, lined up from 20½" to 18½" were retained along with their Joy valve gear. The cab was altered to that used on the Benbow class, and Webb buffers were changed to taper shank type. In most cases a tender of Webb design was retained, only No.1942/5185 being noted as changed to a Whale steel framed type.

Whale's successor Cooke was sufficiently satisfied with the prototype, that he converted two more Jubilees in 1910, and from April 1913, extended the rebuilding to the Benbow class. Ultimately, seventy were done, thirty-seven Jubilees, and thirty-three Benbows, the other three and seven being scrapped whilst still in the compound version.

After the end of the LNWR, the capuchon on the chimney was usually taken off, but in LMS numbering, it was retained by 5110, 5116, 5117, 5121, 5152, 5172, 5176, 5183 and 5186. From 1925, socket lampholders were normally replaced by vertical irons, but some kept sockets until their withdrawal in 1930. No.5179 seems to have been unique in having safety valves changed to pops, and it, along with 1961 and 5110 were recorded as having a boiler on which the washout plugs were visible. Despite the engine's relatively small size, the 7' 0" coupled wheels caused the height of the edges of the cab roof to foul the Midland line load gauge, and five Renowns 5138 (9/28), 5129 (3/29), 5165 (9/29), 5183 (9/29) and 5179 (1/30) were altered to pass that gauge, noticeably by the loss of their rainstrips. In their final LNW years, many had shields fitted to the end of their sandpipes to the driving wheels, to prevent sand being blown away by side winds from where it could be effective, but most had been taken off whilst the engines were still that Company's property. Although the final rebuilding was not until December 1924, withdrawal began as early as April 1925, and was completed by taking the last twelve out of stock in December 1931.

When the LMS renumbering scheme was prepared early in 1923, the fifty-six by then rebuilt as Renowns were allocated 5131 to 5186, but fifteen never had those numbers applied, being withdrawn still bearing LNW number. Twelve of the fourteen rebuilt after Grouping (allocated numbers in 5110-30 range) took their LMS number after rebuilding, the exceptions being 1952/5119 and 1967/5125, scrapped still in LNW numbering.

No Renown was changed to LMS numbering before April 1926 so none were painted red, or had small LMS put on their cab sides. 5127, 5131 and 5176 were so numbered in April 1926, but only by having their brass plates taken off and new number painted in its place, using the same 6" high figures.

Until 1928 (when number was moved from tender to cab) 18" numerals were used on tender, and the 14" circular LMS armorial was put on the cab, 5123, 5157 and 5186 being such examples, although 5186's tender kept its LNW lining.

From early 1928, LMS was put on tender in 14", but cab numerals could be done either in matching 14" (such as 5117, 5141, 5172, 5179 and 5183), or in only 10", of which 5121, 5144, 5155 and 5156 were examples. All except 5127 and 5131 are believed to have had cast numberplate fitted on smokebox door, and retained them to withdrawal. No Renown survived long enough to have its LNW shed allocation plate moved from cab roof.

1901 JUBILEE was rebuilt in April 1919, and although engine here is in plain black, tender is lined. Note sandshields are still fitted. It became LMS 5156 in March 1928 - ***see later photograph.***

RENOWN CLASS 2-CYLINDER SIMPLE REBUILDS from 4-CYLINDER COMPOUNDS

LMS No.	Applied	LNW No.	Date Rebuilt	Withdrawn
5110	6/26	1903	5/24	11/31
(5111)	—	1904	—	5/23
5112	2/28	1911	12/24	12/31
5113	6/26	1912	5/24	11/29
5114	7/26	1915	11/23	7/28
(5115)	—	1923	—	3/25
5116	11/26	1927	1/24	12/31
5117	5/28	1929	2/24	12/30
—	—	1908	—	1/23 as 3648
—	—	1956	—	1/23 as 3647
—	—	1976	—	12/22 as 3644
(5118)	—	1944	—	2/27
(5119)	—	1952	11/23	2/28
5120	12/26	1953	12/23	10/28
5121	3/28	1954	10/24	7/30
(5122)	—	1955	—	8/23 as 3630
5123	10/26	1964	9/24	11/29
(5124)	—	1966	—	4/25
(5125)	—	1967	11/23	2/28
5126	3/27	1969	4/24	4/30
5127	4/26	1970	4/24	11/27
(5128)	—	1974	— (Sup.5/21)	3/28
5129	6/27	1977	2/24	12/30
(5130)	—	1979	—	8/23 as 3631
5131	4/26	1918	6/08	9/28
(5132)	—	1913	3/10	9/28
5133	10/27	1935	3/10	11/29
(5134)	—	1921	4/13	7/26
5135	10/27	1971	4/13	11/30
(5136)	—	1951	10/13	4/25
5137	8/27	1905	8/14	11/30
5138	8/28	1946	10/14	12/31
5139	2/27	1945	9/15	6/30
5140	11/27	1961	9/15	10/28
5141	10/26	1948	10/15	8/30
5142	10/26	1930	4/16	11/30
5143	10/27	1959	4/16	1/30
5144	9/27	1257 (ex1914)	9/16	10/31
5145	11/26	1943	9/16	10/28
(5146)	—	1922	10/16	11/27
(5147)	—	1925	4/17	2/28
5148	9/26	1957	4/17	1/28
5149	2/27	1906	5/17	12/31
(5150)	—	1936	6/17	6/25
(5151)	—	1965	8/17	6/25
5152	1/28	1949	1/18	5/30
5153	10/26	1960	2/18	10/28
5154	11/27	1937	1/19	10/28
5155	1/28	1916	2/19	9/30
5156	3/28	1901	4/19	12/31
5157	1/28	1902	8/19	7/30
5158	8/27	1939	8/19	10/28
(5159)	—	1909	11/19	4/28
5160	6/27	1919	11/19	11/28
5161	11/27	1938	2/20	10/28
(5162)	—	1932	6/20	4/25
5163	11/26	1963	6/20	11/28
5164	1/27	1968	6/20	9/28
5165	7/27	1934	9/20	12/31
5166	8/28	1920	12/20	12/30
5167	11/27	1975	1/21	11/28
(5168)	—	1972	3/21	4/25
(5169)	—	1933	4/21	1/28

LMS No.	Applied	LNW No.	Date Rebuilt	Withdrawn
5170	9/28	1940	4/21	11/29
(5171)	—	1962	6/21	3/26
5172	10/26	1910	8/21	4/31
5173	7/27	1928	8/21	12/31
(5174)	—	1947	9/21	10/25
(5175)	—	1973	9/21	7/26
5176	4/26	1931	12/21	6/30
5177	8/27	1978	12/21	5/30
(5178)	—	1907	2/22	6/26
5179	9/27	1941	2/22	9/31
5180	1/27	1926	3/22	12/31
5181	10/26	1958	4/22	10/28
5182	6/26	1980	5/22	12/31
5183	6/28	1924	6/22	12/31
5184	7/27	1917	8/22	12/31
5185	9/26	1942	9/22	2/30
5186	10/27	1950	10/22	12/31

1902 BLACK PRINCE was rebuilt in August 1919 from Jubilee class, and kept a chimney with capuchon, despite getting a 4" diameter bigger boiler. Here in unlined black, in January 1928 it became LMS 5157, and it was withdrawn in July 1930.

1943 QUEEN ALEXANDRA changed from Benbow to Renown class in September 1916 but lost its lining at a later shopping, and here is plain black. Without capuchon it has had a buffer type change and from November 1926 it was LMS 5145 and was withdrawn in October 1928.

1946 DIADEM rebuilt in October 1914, was duly lined out, but here has had its tender changed to one in plain black. In August 1928, it was renumbered LMS 5138, and had its cab roof edges modified so as to pass MR gauge. With all the other eleven survivors, it was withdrawn in December 1931.

5110 IRON DUKE was not rebuilt to Renown class until May 1924 and then kept LNW 1903 until June 1926. Seen at Edge Hill it has a boiler on which the washout plugs can be seen, but the sockets have been replaced by LMS lampirons. It was in the 12 withdrawn in December 1931 which made the class extinct.

5179 ALFRED THE GREAT became a Renown in February 1922, but here at Bletchley on 30th August 1930 with boiler showing plugs, has also changed to Ross pop safety valves. Changed in September 1927 from LNW 1941 it then had emblem put on cab, but in January 1930 its cab was modified to pass MR gauge, one of only five so recorded.
A.B.Crompton.

1257 INVINCIBLE takes on water at Manchester (London Road) after turning. The engine was re-numbered from 1914 in April 1920 so that the war memorial engine could have that number, and was the only one of the class to change LNW number. It was rebuilt in September 1916 when the sandshields would be fitted, and this view shows the lamp sockets clearly. In September 1927 it became LMS 5144 - ***see later photo.***

5117 POLYPHEMUS had been LNW 1929 until March 1928, although it had become a Renown in February 1924. Here at Rugby, as well as buffer change it has also changed to lamp irons. Withdrawal was in December 1930.

1951 BACCHANTE became a Renown in October 1913 when this lining was standard application. Here it has one of the earlier Webb 1800 gallon tenders which had tie rods to the axleboxes. It was to have been LMS 5136 but was withdrawn in April 1925 without acquiring that number.

1961 ALBEMARLE changed to Renown class in September 1915, and here in wartime unlined black, it has a 2000 gallon Webb tender with bar framing instead of tie rod, and also equal axle spacing. Note its boiler has plugs visible. In November 1927 it became LMS 5140 but then only survived until October 1928 withdrawal. *Real Photos.*

5185 KING EDWARD VII was LNW 1942 until September 1926 when emblem was put on its cab, having become a Renown in September 1922. Note that it has a Whale tender with steel frame and two open coal rails, and here it is at Crewe station in 1929 before withdrawal in February 1930, but still retains LNW lamp sockets. *W.L.Good.*

5152 KING ARTHUR in January 1928 would be about the last to get the circular emblem, and number on the tender, which it took from LNW 1949, already a Renown from January 1918. LMS renumbering of Renowns did not start until April 1926, so none were painted red, or got LMS lettering on cab. 5152 was withdrawn in May 1930.

5186 VICTORIOUS, a Renown from October 1922, kept LNW 1950 until October 1927, and then got this style, which it then probably kept until withdrawn in December 1931. Here it is at Crewe North shed.

5121 GALATEA, rebuilt in October 1924 remained as LNW 1954 until March 1928, when the cast plates were taken off and 10" figures were put in their place. Withdrawn July 1930, it kept sockets.

The class leader RENOWN changed from LNWR 1918 to LMS 5131 in April 1926 but suffered the indignity of simply having its number plates removed and replaced by only 6 inch painted figures. The engine retained its LNW paint and lining but the tender is unlined. Here it is looking rather shabby at Preston.

5155 IRRESISTIBLE was rebuilt in February 1919 as LNW 1916 which it kept until January 1928. It then lost its cast plates which were superseded by this 10" figuring, and that was retained until withdrawal in September 1930. In the early part of that year it was stabled at Brunswick (Liverpool) shed.

5156 JUBILEE rebuilt in April 1919 kept LNW 1901 until March 1928 when its cab plates were removed and these 10" figures put on. Note it was one which did change to lamp irons before withdrawal in December 1931. The diamond at each end of the name is still visible.

5141 CAMPERDOWN was rebuilt to a Renown in October 1915 but did not change to its LMS number until October 1926. Shopped after the January 1928 ruling to put number on cab, it was given the orthodox style of 14" numbers.

1937 SUPERB was rebuilt from Benbow to Renown class in January 1919 and here in 1920 is pilot to 1973 HOOD, still in Benbow class, on a Bangor to Manchester express at Colwyn Bay.

1958 ROYAL OAK, a Renown class from April 1922 leads nameless 440 of Prince of Wales class on a down express approaching Crewe in 1922. The Renown has both engine and tender in LNW lining and the armorial on the splasher can still be discerned. *Real Photos.*

1980 NEPTUNE here in 1924 piloting unnamed Claughton 5996 is on an up main line express. *A.G.Ellis.*

1978 MERLIN on this up express milk train for London is at Shilton, south of Nuneaton. A change of tender is very noticeable from the difference in their paint. *LGRP.*

5116 GOLIATH on a stopping passenger train. Note that no Renown class was ever fitted with Beames oilboxes on the boiler handrails.

WHALE'S 4-4-0 "PRECURSOR" CLASS

When Whale became C.M.E. in 1903, he was faced with main line needs to improve the erratic performance of a hundred 3-cylinder compounds, all with divided drive. There were also seventy of the 4-cylinder 4-4-0 compounds, with another ten of them under construction. The regular provision of a pilot engine for them was a waste of resources, and he was determined to run the main line trains more effectively. As a Running Superintendent he had direct experience of how unreliable the compounds could be, so he quickly began to replace them with a basic, well-tried design. His Precursor class proved both resolute and reliable, so in $3\frac{1}{2}$ years, Crewe built 130 of them. That enabled the 100 divided drive compounds to be ruthlessly swept away, even if he did follow tradition on the LNWR by perpetuating many of their names. When he retired at the end of February 1909, his successor inherited main line locomotives which could fully support the claim that the London & North Western Railway was indeed "The Premier Line".

The basic "Precursor" design turned out so well that both Whale, and Cooke, were each able to develop it into two other very successful classes, Whale with the Experiments and the 19" Goods, and Cooke with the George the Fifth, and Prince of Wales classes. Both were also able to introduce a powerful passenger tank engine based on it. Despite Webb's predilection and persistence with compounds, it is only fair to mention that the Precursor was just a more powerful version of Webb's 2-4-0 Jumbo class.

When the LMS was formed, eighty Precursors were still running as they were built, and to them numbers 5187 to 5266 were allocated, although seven were withdrawn from November 1927 to February 1928 without having new numbers applied. The other fifty were developed more powerfully in two stages, the first being simply to change them from saturated to superheated steam, the first so done - in February 1913 - being No.513 PRECURSOR itself. Another eleven were altered similarly from January 1917 to September 1919, of which three (by boiler exchange) reverted to saturated during 1929/30. All of the others except 5270 proceeded to the further improvement in which the superheating was accompanied by rebuilding from slide to piston valves and $20\frac{1}{2}$" instead of 19" cylinders. To those fifty the LMS allocated numbers 5270 to 5319, all of which were duly applied. Of those remaining as built, withdrawal began in October 1927 and that variety was extinct when 5235 was taken out of stock in April 1935, and none of them survived to have 20,000 added to their number.

From new, capuchon on chimney was usual, but some did run without it later, No.1 and 2585 being examples of plain chimney top, both of them in 1920.

513 PRECURSOR, the initial engine of the class, here in Euston about 1909 depicts the straightforward appearance of the class. Webb items which were retained included Ramsbottom safety valves, capuchon on chimney, socket lampholders, displacement lubricator on smokebox side, and the glossy black fully lined painting. The driving wheels reverted to small boss, two washout plugs were fitted on each side, taper-shank buffers and steel plate were introduced, and the tender was up-dated. Now of 3000 gallons, and all steel framing, axles were equally spaced on 6' 9" centres. Coal rails were cut from three to two, but tool boxes were retained on top of the tender front. *E.T.Vyse.*

In August 1920, No.2585 was fitted with Scarab oil fuel firing for trials, which included a Euston to Birmingham (New St) run, but that equipment was then soon discarded, and 2585 was seen later to have a capuchon again, by then as LMS 5236. In the later LNW years many were fitted with sandshields, close to rail level, but they proved very vulnerable to damage, and very few survived into LMS days. From 1925 the socket lampholders were gradually changed to vertical irons, and another visible difference of detail was the use of Ross pop safety valves in place of the Ramsbottom type. Replacement boilers had four, instead of two washout plugs on each side of their firebox. When new, all were coupled with a new design of tender, which was steel framed, and had two open coal rails, but there were frequent changes to the three later tender types which were introduced by Whale's successor.

Of the eighty which remained in original condition, only two were recorded as being given LMS red livery, both after Crewe Paint Shop re-started following the total re-organisation of that Works. In November 1926, Nos. 5193 and 5201 were reported to have received red painting, and prior to the number being moved on to the cab from January 1928, at least 5204 and 5252 carried the circular emblem there, with eighteen inch numerals on the tender. No.5224 also had the emblem, but its tender was plain, and the engine number was applied only by a cast plate on the smokebox door.

303 HIMALAYA was one of twelve superheated from February 1913 to September 1919 but not rebuilt with piston valves; altered in January 1919 it kept its short smokebox. Note sandshields to both wheels, and photograph is 1921 or later, because of full lining, and fitting of Beames oil box on the boiler handrail. It was one of the few on which the armorial was also restored post-war. *Real Photos.*

2585 WATT was fitted in August 1920 for Scarab oil fuel firing and ran trials between London and Birmingham, but it was the only one so equipped, and the experiment was soon terminated. Note that it has been changed to coupled wheels with large boss, and there is no capuchon on the chimney.

PRECURSOR CLASS STILL AS BUILT AT END OF L.N.W.R.

LNW No.	NAME	Built	Rebuilt	LMS No.	Applied	To 2XXXX	Withdrawn
2023	*HELVELLYN*	4/04	3/24	5187	6/26	11/34	3/36
412	*ALFRED PAGET* *(MARQUIS from 11/04)*	6/04	3/23	5188	4/26	10/34	4/40
510	*ALBATROSS*	6/04	—	5189	7/28	—	8/33
639	*AJAX*	10/04	—	5190	11/26	—	9/28
648	*ARCHIMEDES*	10/04	—	5191	2/27	—	1/28
685	*COSSACK*	10/04	—	5192	11/26	—	4/32
1102	*THUNDERBOLT*	11/04	—	5193	11/26	—	9/31
1117	*VANDAL*	11/04	—	5194	2/26	—	10/31
622	*EUPHRATES*	12/04	—	(5195)	—	—	11/27
638	*HUSKISSON*	12/04	—	5196	7/27	—	4/33
645	*MAMMOTH*	1/05	—	5197	5/27	—	11/30
40	*NIAGARA*	3/05	—	5198	1/28	—	11/30
1104	*CEDRIC*	2/05	—	5199	8/28	—	12/33
1111	*CERBERUS*	3/05	—	5200	2/26	—	9/34
1431	*EGERIA*	3/05	—	5201	11/26	—	11/30
520	*PANOPEA*	3/05	—	5202	8/27	—	1/34
2031	*WAVERLEY*	3/05	—	5203	4/27	—	11/31
184	*HAVELOCK*	5/05	—	5204	6/27	—	9/31
1115	*APOLLO*	4/05	—	5205	6/26	—	2/28
1545	*CYCLOPS*	4/05	—	5206	10/27	—	5/32
2061	*EGLINTON*	4/05	3/25	5207	8/27	11/34	8/36
519	*MESSENGER*	5/05	—	5208	10/27	—	11/31
2120	*TRENTHAM*	5/05	—	(5209)	—	—	10/27
1430	*VICTOR*	5/05	—	5210	9/27	—	10/31
113	*AURANIA*	7/05	12/24	5211	11/27	11/34	9/36
315	*HARROWBY*	7/05	4/23	5212	2/27	11/34	12/36
311	*EMPEROR*	9/05	—	5213	9/27	—	5/33
1509	*AMERICA*	7/05	—	5214	5/26	—	3/28
2257	*VULTURE*	8/05	—	5215	2/27	—	12/33
911	*HERALD*	9/05	3/24	5216	9/27	11/34	2/36
1114	*KNOWSLEY*	9/05	—	5217	11/26	—	2/33
1116	*PANDORA*	9/05	4/23	5218	2/26	11/34	4/36
1510	*PSYCHE*	9/05	—	5219	10/27	—	12/30
1784	*PYTHON*	10/05	—	5220	10/27	—	11/31
2202	*VIZIER*	10/05	—	5221	6/27	—	12/30
117	*ALASKA*	10/05	—	5222	10/27	—	9/33
127	*SNAKE*	11/05	3/23	5223	4/28	11/34	11/36
229	*STORK*	11/05	—	(5224)	—	—	11/27
1301	*CANDIDATE*	10/05	5/25	5225	12/26	5/36	11/36
1396	*HARPY*	11/05	—	5226	12/27	—	11/30
2007	*OREGON*	11/05	—	(5227)	—	—	10/27
2012	*PENGUIN*	11/05	—	5228	5/28	—	10/31
2115	*SERVIA*	11/05	—	5229	5/27	—	4/32
2576	*ARAB*	12/05	—	5230	10/26	—	9/33
2579	*GANYMEDE*	12/05	2/25	5231	6/27	—	2/36
2580	*PROBLEM*	12/05	—	5232	5/28	—	11/31
2581	*PEEL*	12/05	—	5233	11/26	—	8/34
2582	*ROWLAND HILL*	12/05	—	5234	12/26	—	11/28
2583	*TEUTONIC* *(THE TSAR from 11/14)* *(MOONSTONE from 12/15)*	12/05	—	5235	4/28	—	4/35
2585	*WATT*	1/06	—	5236	9/27	—	12/33
234	*PEARL*	3/06	—	5237	12/27	—	2/32
526	*ILION*	3/06	—	5238	12/26	—	12/28
723	*COPTIC*	2/06	7/23	5239	1/28	—	1/36
837	*FRIAR*	2/06	—	5240	12/27	—	10/33
1311	*NAPOLEON*	3/06	4/23	5241	8/28	—	1/36
1312	*IONIC*	2/06	—	5242	3/27	—	11/30
1642	*LAPWING*	3/06	5/24	5243	1/28	—	11/35
2017	*TUBAL*	3/06	11/26	5244	11/26	—	11/35
561	*ANTAEUS*	4/06	12/24	5245	1/27	4/36	3/41
675	*ADJUTANT*	4/06	6/26	5246	6/26	—	2/36

LNW No.	NAME	Built	Rebuilt	LMS No.	Applied	To 2XXXX	Withdrawn
772	*ADMIRAL*	4/06	—	(5247)	—	—	10/27
804	*AMPHION*	4/06	3/23	5248	6/27	—	10/35
988	*BELLEROPHON*	4/06	----	5249	9/26	—	6/33
1433	*FAERIE QUEENE*	4/06	3/25	5250	6/27	—	11/35
1650	*RICHARD TREVITHICK*	5/06	—	(5251)	—	—	2/28
1787	*HYPERION*	5/06	—	5252	2/27	—	12/30
1	*CLIVE*	6/07	—	5253	8/28	—	11/30
218	*DAPHNE*	6/07	—	5254	11/26	—	8/33
419	*MONARCH*	6/07	—	5255	5/28	—	12/30
665	*MERSEY*	6/07	—	(5256)	—	—	10/27
1011	*LOCKE*	7/07	—	5257	11/27	—	1/33
1364	*CLYDE*	7/07	—	5258	10/26	—	11/30
2053	*EDITH*	7/07	—	5259	11/27	—	3/34
2181	*ELEANOR*	7/07	—	5260	1/28	—	12/33
276	*DORIC*	7/07	—	5261	12/26	—	11/27
754	*CELTIC*	7/07	—	5262	8/27	—	12/30
807	*OCEANIC*	8/07	—	5263	11/26	—	12/33
976	*PACIFIC*	8/07	—	5264	11/26	—	11/28
1297	*PHALARIS*	8/07	—	5265	5/27	—	10/31
1516	*ALECTO*	8/07	—	5266	5/28	—	10/31

LMS numbers 5267, 5268 and 5269 were never used.

218 DAPHNE, here at Llandudno on 29th July 1920 shows some of the minor modifications made to Precursors. The sheet steel shields at the front of the bogie were uncommon as Precursors were usually pilots and not piloted. The buffers are the 1' 7½" Cooke design instead of Whale's 1' 4½" length. Note Cooke sandshields fitted to rear coupled wheels, and pipe modified to carry one on leading wheels. *LCGB Ken Nunn Collection.*

No.1 CLIVE, post 1922. It has regained capuchon, but the sandshields previously fitted have gone. The Beames oil box on the boiler handrail has been added. Fully lined livery, which it lost at a late 1920 shopping, has been restored and which it then carried to August 1928 when it became LMS 5253, but tender type is changed. Now it has one built for a George V, with double beaded top, formerly it had one with two open rails. Tool boxes had been replaced by built-in cupboards lower down.

685 COSSACK is coupled with a 1916 designed tender by Cooke which had square ends to the frame, in which the openings had parallel top and bottom with semi-circular ends. The coping had also been changed to a single beading. *Real Photos.*

5252 HYPERION was LNW 1787 to February 1927, but at that shopping its sockets were replaced by LMS type lamp irons, and its safety valves were now Ross pop type.

When 5254 DAPHNE changed to that LMS number in November 1926, and got emblem, a plain black tender was coupled to it, and the only sign of its number was the plate on its smokebox door. Note the replacement 4-plug boiler, but still with Ramsbottom safety valves.

638 HUSKISSON has one of the original boilers with Ramsbottom safety valves and two washout plugs on each side of the firebox. Note that a short horizontal handrail has been added on the cab. It is in the black painting without lining used in 1917-21. On some of the original boilers *(see 5236/52)* the LMS changed the safety valves to Ross pop type.

None of those which remained in Precursor class changed to LMS numbering until February 1926, so none were painted red or got LMS put on cab. No.1104 CEDRIC was not altered until August 1928 when it became 5199, but in 1926 it was coupled with red tender 5290 so painted in September 1923. The engine's only change of detail is the addition of Beames oil boxes on the boiler handrails.

5210 VICTOR had been LNW 1430 until September 1927 when emblem was put on a cab in unlined black, but number was on a tender which had LNW lining. Its replacement boiler has four plugs and also Ross pops, and lamp sockets have been replaced by irons.

5236 WATT got its LMS number in September 1927, then later, had it put on the cab as here just before December 1933 withdrawal. Both engine and tender are unlined, but LMS is faintly visible, and smokebox number plate has been removed. Note LNW shedplate 10 (Monument Lane) moved from cab roof to smokebox door. As this class was extinct in April 1935, none got the LMS cast plate introduced in January 1935.

5202 had been LNW 520 until August 1927, and here on a Barrow to Carnforth stopping train at Grange-over-Sands, has its number on the cab, but only in 10" figures. Note that its replacement boiler, although with four washout plugs, is one still with safety valves of Ramsbottom type. Others to get 10" figures were 5208 and 5220 in October and 5226 in December 1927.
N.E.Preedy Collection.

622 EUPHRATES at Camden shed in 1915 has had coupled wheels changed to large boss type as used by George the Fifth class. Note sandshields fitted to both coupled wheels, and that the lubricator has been removed from the base of the smokebox. 622 did not change to LMS number and in November 1927 was one of the first to be withdrawn.
LNWR Society.

806 SWIFTSURE, here at Runcorn, has the 12 noon express from Liverpool (Lime St) to Taunton and Swansea. The engine is still in original condition, with displacement lubricator on the side of the smokebox.

5260 ELEANOR from January 1928 here is on the main line nearing Oxenholme with a stopping train from Carlisle including a Keswick portion, and two milk tanks. Its boiler with four plugs has Ross safety valves. Note LNW shedplate 27 (Preston) moved from cab to smokebox door, so the picture is later than January 1931. *Lens of Sutton..*

2181 ELEANOR is pilot to another of the class about to leave Euston on a West Coast main line express about 1919. It has one of the tenders introduced in 1916, and is in the 1917-21 unlined black painting. The train engine has lined livery, and one of the tenders with two coal rails built for the Precursors.

2585 WATT in September 1920 fitted for oil fuel fitting, is climbing Camden bank on an express from London to Birmingham (New St).

In LMS years, extensive use of this class was made as pilots, and here on Dillicar troughs 5266 ALECTO is assisting a former L&Y 4-6-0 on an Aberdeen to London meat train in 1929.
Real Photos.

5228 PENGUIN at Bletchley on 30th August 1930 shows its final condition at November 1931 withdrawal. Alterations have been to pop safety valves, to lamp irons, to large boss coupled wheels, and to a later design of tender. Not given its LMS number until May 1928, it does not appear to have had a smokebox number plate fitted.
A.B.Crompton.

5194 VANDAL at Crewe station on 13th March 1926 still in LNW painting but with numberplate removed in February and the LMS number stencilled in its place. Note no smokebox plate has been fitted, and it had not yet acquired Beames oil boxes.

PRECURSOR CLASS FITTED WITH SUPERHEATER

At the end of the LNWR on 31st December 1922, eighty of the 130 Precursors were still using saturated steam and had slide valves. To these the LMS gave their numbers 5187 to 5266, then did not use 5267/8/9. Numbers 5270 to 5275 were allocated to six engines which had been superheated in May and June 1918, but of which five had not been rebuilt to piston valves. No.1363's conversion also to piston valves was overlooked in the LMS renumbering to 5272. The five slide valve engines also kept short smokebox, but were fitted with mechanical lubricator, mounted on the right hand frame plate. 5274 was rebuilt with piston valves and 6" smaller bogie wheels by the LMS, and from July 1929 to June 1930, Nos.5271/3/5 reverted to using saturated steam through boiler exchange. 5270 however kept superheated steam but remained a slide valve engine to its May 1936 withdrawal, which then made the slide valve variety extinct.

As with those retaining saturated steam and slide valves, buffers could be either the 1' 4½" Whale or 1' 7½" Cooke length, and socket lampholders generally were replaced by irons. Beames oil boxes with five feeds were added on each boiler handrail, and there was a change from Ramsbottom to Ross pop safety valves. Boiler replacements on 5270 and 5275 had Belpaire firebox, and tenders of three different types could be seen coupled with them. Only 5270 and 5275 seem to have changed to coupled wheels with large boss.

Re-numbering to 5273 and to 5275 was as early as March 1924, both then being painted red with yellow lining, and having small LMS on cab, with 18" numerals on tender. It is not known how 5270/71 were treated when they were changed to those numbers in August 1926 and July 1927. From 1928 all four were in unlined black with 14" number on the cab and LMS on the tender, and remained so to withdrawal.

5273 reverted to saturated in July 1929, and without the superheater, the mechanical lubricator was not needed, so was also taken off as seen at Shrewsbury in August 1929. *C.A.J.Nevett.*

PRECURSOR CLASS REBUILT WITH SUPERHEATER, PISTON VALVES & 20½" CYLINDERS.

Between January 1913 and January 1923, Crewe superheated and rebuilt to piston valve forty-four Precursors, and Crewe continued the process under LMS auspices from March 1923 until November 1926 on an additional eighteen. To the forty-four already done the LMS gave numbers 5276 to 5319, and the later eighteen had already been allocated numbers in the 5187 to 5266 series. Of these eighteen, only the two done in 1926 (LNW 675/5246 and 2017/5244) got their LMS numbers at the time of rebuilding; the other sixteen retained LNW number and painting, two of them for no less than five years. No.127 SNAKE rebuilt in March 1923 only became 5223 in April 1928, whilst 1311 NAPOLEON rebuilt in April 1923 did not become 5244 until August 1928.

These rebuilds were then equivalent to the George the Fifth class, but could be readily identified, because they kept separate splasher to their driving wheels. They differed from Precursors by having smokebox extended from 3' 7" to 5' 0" long, and because of their 1½" bigger cylinders and piston valves, the bogie wheels had to be changed to 3' 3" instead of 3' 9" diameter.

At the end of 1939 only seven (25277, 25292, 25297, 25300, 25304, 25311 and 25319) survived, and at the end of the LMS 25297 was the only one left to be handed on to British Railways. When that was withdrawn in June 1949, all the 130 which had begun as a Precursor were extinct, and none got any indication of nationalised ownership.

The original equipment included 1' 4½" long buffers, socket lampholders, capuchon on chimney, round-top firebox, Ramsbottom safety valves, coupled wheels with small boss, no short horizontal handrail on cab side, no windshields, wheel and handle to fasten smokebox door, and tender with two open coal rails. Subsequent change was made to all ten of these items, in addition to which, all were fitted by Beames with additional oil box at each side, mounted on the boiler handrail.

PRECURSOR CLASS AS SUPERHEATED, AND ALSO REBUILT WITH PISTON VALVES

LNW No.	NAME	Built	Super-heated	Piston valves	LMS No.	Applied	To 2XXXX	With-drawn
469	*MARMION*	6/07	5/18	—	5270	8/26	4/34	5/36
802	*GAELIC*	7/07	5/18	—	5271	7/27	—	11/31
1363	*CORNWALL (BRINDLEY from 5/11)*	10/05	5/18	5/18	5272	8/27	10/36	12/39
2064	*JASON*	3/05	5/18	—	5273	3/24	—	8/31
688	*HECATE*	7/05	6/18	3/23	5274	6/27	—	10/35
1439	*TIGER*	11/05	6/18	—	5275	3/24	—	1/33
7	*TITAN*	6/04	1/13	1/13	5276	4/28	—	10/35
2164	*OBERON*	4/04	1/13	1/13	5277	11/27	9/36	8/46
513	*PRECURSOR*	3/04	2/13	1/15	5278	5/27	—	7/36
2062	*SUNBEAM*	8/05	2/13	2/13	5279	10/27	6/36	8/39
2166	*SHOOTING STAR*	10/05	2/13	2/13	5280	5/27	—	11/35
564	*EREBUS*	6/07	9/13	9/13	5281	9/27	—	9/36
515	*CHAMPION*	12/04	9/13	9/13	5282	11/27	6/36	12/39
2011	*BROUGHAM*	8/07	9/13	9/13	5283	8/27	—	3/36
333	*AMBASSADOR*	12/04	11/13	11/13	5284	2/24	8/36	8/36
1419	*TAMERLANE*	3/04	11/13	11/13	5285	8/26	—	3/36
1573	*DUNROBIN*	4/05	4/14	4/14	5286	4/26	5/36	9/37
365	*ALCHYMIST*	4/05	5/14	5/14	5287	12/27	5/36	6/37
1469	*TANTALUS*	3/05	5/14	5/14	5288	2/27	11/36	3/37
301	*LEVIATHAN*	11/04	6/14	6/14	5289	9/27	—	5/36
310	*ACHILLES*	12/04	6/14	6/14	5290	9/23	—	10/36
1395	*HARBINGER*	3/04	9/14	9/14	5291	3/27	12/36	6/37
366	*MEDUSA*	5/05	11/14	11/14	5292	7/26	12/36	4/45
2513	*LEVENS*	3/06	11/14	11/14	5293	7/27	12/36	6/39
106	*DRUID*	10/04	12/14	12/14	5294	1/28	12/36	5/37
1723	*SCORPION*	8/05	12/14	12/14	5295	5/27	—	11/36
659	*DREADNOUGHT*	6/04	1/15	1/15	5296	3/24	—	5/36
643*	*SIROCCO*	11/04	3/15	3/15	5297	11/27	12/36	6/49
60	*DRAGON*	10/04	4/15	4/15	5298	4/27	9/36	11/38
1137	*VESUVIUS*	2/05	4/15	4/15	5299	4/27	5/36	8/36
1617	*HYDRA*	8/05	5/15	5/15	5300	1/28	12/36	6/40
300	*EMERALD*	7/05	1/17	1/17	5301	2/28	—	10/35
1309	*SHAMROCK*	8/07	1/17	11/22	5302	4/28	9/36	6/37
323	*ARGUS*	2/05	6/17	1/23	5303	2/27	---	10/36
302	*GREYHOUND*	7/05	7/17	7/22	5304	1/27	8/36	1/47
303	*HIMALAYA*	1/05	1/19	6/28	5305	6/28	—	1/36
1287	*LANG MEG*	3/06	9/19	5/26	5306	4/28	—	2/36
305	*SENATOR*	11/04	6/20	6/20	5307	4/28	1/37	2/37
2	*SIMOOM*	6/04	8/20	8/20	5308	10/27	—	10/36
2578	*FAME*	12/05	8/20	8/20	5309	10/23	—	8/36
1120	*THUNDERER (taken off 9/36)*	1/05	10/21	10/21	5310	6/26	7/36	8/39
811	*EXPRESS (taken off 9/36)*	9/05	11/21	11/21	5311	11/27	12/36	3/41
2584	*VELOCIPEDE (taken off 8/33)*	1/06	1/22	1/22	5312	5/27	—	12/35
2577	*ETNA*	12/05	2/22	2/22	5313	8/27	—	2/36
282	*ALARIC*	4/06	4/22	4/22	5314	2/28	—	11/35
2051	*DELAMERE*	8/07	6/22	6/22	5315	4/26	—	9/36
1737	*VISCOUNT*	3/05	10/22	10/22	5316	3/27	—	7/36
374	*EMPRESS*	9/05	12/22	12/22	5317	9/27	—	6/36
806	*SWIFTSURE*	1/05	1/23	1/23	5318	5/26	—	10/35
990	*BUCEPHALUS*	4/06	1/23	1/23	5319	7/27	5/36	12/40

** BR 58010 allotted March 1948 but not applied.*

Superheater removed from 5271 (6/30), 5273 (7/29) and 5275 (4/30).

5273, at Camden shed, as painted red in March 1924, and showing mechanical lubricator fitted when superheater added in May 1918. Note boiler has four wash-out plugs, and Beames 5-feed oilbox has been added.

5275 at Edge Hill shed Liverpool on 25th April 1925, still in red livery, has changed to Belpaire firebox, Ross pop safety valves, wheels with large boss, and 1916 design tender with frame edge vertical at rear end. It has also had Beames oil box and short horizontal handrail on cab added.

25272 was so numbered from October 1936 to its December 1939 withdrawal, and the 6" smaller bogie wheels confirm that it had been changed from slide to piston valves.

1419 TAMERLANE at Manchester (London Road) in 1914 has capuchon which was standard on the class. Damper gear is fitted (operated througfh the boiler handrail) but was removed later as not necessary, which also applied to the sandshields to the coupled wheels. *LNWR Society.*

2166 SHOOTING STAR rebuilt in February 1913 gained mechanical lubricator and pyrometer in connection with superheating, and also got sandshields. It was also changed to wheels with large boss. Note it has only five fixing bolts for the cylinders and the tender has been changed to one of the George the Fifth type. *A.G.Ellis.*

365 ALCHYMIST was rebuilt in May 1914, and here has a replacement boiler with four plugs, no pyrometer or sandshields, and has changed to large boss wheels but still has tender with 2 open coal rails.

1433 FAERIE QUEENE was not rebuilt until April 1925 but then kept LNW numbering and lining on tender until it became 5250 in June 1927. It also kept boiler with two plugs and Ramsbottom safety valves. Here it is at Camden shed on 2nd May 1925. *LCGB Ken Nunn Coll.*

5296 DREADNOUGHT was rebuilt in January 1915 as LNW 659 and it got LMS numbering, and red painting in March 1924. Note boiler with four plugs but Ramsbottom safety valves, also Beames oilboxes have been added, but it still lacks a cross rail on the cab.

412 MARQUIS was rebuilt in March 1923 and kept LNW livery; then in April 1926, its number plates were removed and 6" 5188 painted on cab. Later, it changed to this red tender, with 'Prince of Wales' class number, the LMS armorial covered the cab number and the LNW crest on the splasher was blacked out; presumably cast number 5188 was put on smokebox door. In April 1926, 5286 and 5315 also lost LNW brass number plates, and got those LMS numbers in 6" painted figures.

5239 COPTIC was rebuilt in July 1923 but remained LNW 723 until January 1928, then got these 10" figures and a cast plate on smoke box door. Note replacement boiler with 4 plugs, but it kept Ramsbottom safety valves and small boss coupled wheels. By 30th August 1930 it had 14" numbers.

5299 VESUVIUS here at Rugby on 18th February 1934 appears to be the last to have a boiler with Ramsbottom safety valves. It became 25299 in May 1936, but was then withdrawn in August 1936. *W.L.Good.*

5225 at Rugby on 21st October 1934 has had its CANDIDATE nameplate removed temporarily, because it was not withdrawn until November 1936. Its mechanical lubricator is of different type and mounting. Its LNW 3 shed plate shows it was allocated to Bletchley. *W.L.Good.*

25297 SIROCCO was last of class and here at Crewe Works on 19th June 1949 has just been withdrawn. It was the only one to be changed to two handles for fastening the smokebox door. Note change to Stanier design buffers.

25304 GREYHOUND was so numbered from August 1936 and then still had LNW chimney and a 1905 design tender with two open coal rails, but had been changed to Stanier buffers. *N.E.Preedy Collection.*

25310 lost its THUNDERER name in September 1936 and was nameless to withdrawal in August 1939. The name was needed for a new 5XP class No.5703.

25304 GREYHOUND which survived to January 1947 was changed to a Stanier chimney, but kept wheel and handle on smokebox door.

5283 BROUGHAM from August 1927, here at Rugby on 27th September 1931 has the 3" longer buffers than originally fitted to it as Precursor No.2011. Both were taper-shank type with circular flange. *W.L.Good.*

25311 also lost its EXPRESS name in September 1936 so that it could be used on new 5XP No.5706. The 2XXXX addition to the number made in December 1936 was done by the shed which explains the off-centring. LMS shed plate shows it allocated to Patricroft. *R.S.Carpenter.*

5284 AMBASSADOR, at Camden shed, got this red livery in February 1924 with 18" numbers put on a 1916 design tender. It had been rebuilt in November 1913, and was an early recipient of cross rail on cab. *Real Photos.*

(below) **5290 ACHILLES still in red, has here changed tender to one painted black and numbered for G1 class 0-8-0 No.9229 which took that number in October 1925. Note this early change on the engine from sockets to lamp irons.**

25188 MARQUIS was altered from 5188 as here in October 1934 and was still as depicted when seen at Stafford on 19th July 1936. *W.L.Good.*

25188 ex works in September 1937 had its number centred again on the cab but was mistakenly fitted with ANTAEUS name plates from 25245 and was only corrected to MARQUIS in the following November.

25245 ANTAEUS had correctly positioned number from April 1936, and after losing name plates to 25188, had them restored in November 1937. Note wedge lifting bogie rear wheel clear of rail - purpose unknown.

(below) **5295 SCORPION approaching Crewe on 20th September 1930 piloting Prince of Wales class 5684 ARABIC, has been changed to a tender from an R.O.D. engine, the only one of this class so recorded.**

5313 ETNA is at Northampton on 7th May 1934 having arrived on the 4.00 p.m. semi-fast from Euston. It then took the 5.50 p.m. local pasenger to Rugby.

5309's red painted tender here in 1927 has been transferred to 5292 MEDUSA which got that number in July 1926 and was in unlined black but with emblem on cab. The cab roof edges have been altered to suit Midland line load gauge; those on 5295, behind, have not.

Large boss balance weight spread over five spokes and crescent shape, on 5315 at Northampton on 30th July 1932. *W.L.Good.*

Small boss trailing wheel balance weight limited to four spokes. Few photographs show this because to get it the coupling rod could not be seen which was anathema to the cameramen.

Small boss driving wheel balance weight limited to four spokes, and with square ends, on 5312 VELOCIPEDE before it became nameless in August 1933.

Small boss trailing wheel balance weight limited to two spokes, on 5280 SHOOTING STAR at Shrewsbury in 1935.

5296 DREADNOUGHT piloting a Claughton on the troughs at Brock between Lancaster and Preston in 1927 with the non-stop *ROYAL SCOT* between Carnforth and London (Euston). *A.G.Ellis.*

25297 SIROCCO on 17th June 1947 with a Bettws-y-Coed to Llandudno stopping train, and carrying 7A (Llandudno Junction) shed plate. *C.F.H.Oldham.*

(above) **5311 EXPRESS hauling down coal empties, and picking up water from the troughs at Hatch End, between Pinner and Bushey.**

(left) **25187 HELVELLYN on 4th August 1935 is at Uttoxeter with a class C van train returning empty milk churns from London. Note the LMS 2A (Rugby) shed plate.** *A.B.Crompton.*

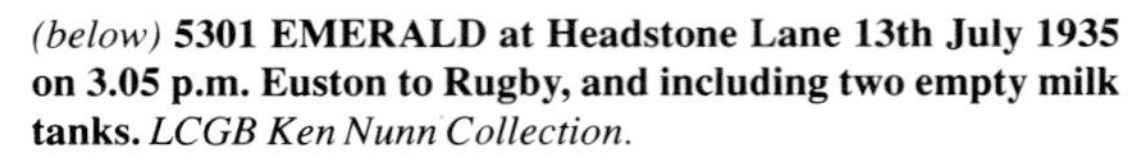

(below) **5301 EMERALD at Headstone Lane 13th July 1935 on 3.05 p.m. Euston to Rugby, and including two empty milk tanks.** *LCGB Ken Nunn Collection.*

GEORGE THE FIFTH 4-4-0 EXPRESS PASSENGER ENGINES

Bowen Cooke was a lucky man; when he became C.M.E. in 1909, his predecessor Whale had already eliminated Webb compounds from main line duties, and replaced them by the completely reliable, and competent, Precursor and Experiment classes. Cooke also took charge just when the benefit to be obtained by superheating was becoming appreciated. The economical effect it could have in reducing coal and water consumption, also giving more power, was amply demonstrated in the exchange he initiated, in autumn 1909, when a London Brighton & South Coast Railway 4-4-2 tank engine was used on the *Sunny South Express* between Brighton and Rugby, in both directions. The result was Crewe being set to work quickly on a superheated version of the Precursor class.

Two engines were completed at Crewe in June 1910, identical except that No.2663 GEORGE THE FIFTH was superheated, and No.2664 QUEEN MARY was not. To make sure the cost of superheating was justified, and that it did not rest on the performance of only one engine, in October/November 1910, Crewe turned out nine more Queen Mary class, and then in November 1910 to January 1911, another nine George the Fifth class. The result was soon apparent; all the further seventy came out with superheater, and the ten Queen Mary class were so fitted from June 1913 to October 1914. When first superheated, all had a damper, operated through the handrail along the left hand (driver's) side, and a pyrometer connection to the cab on the right hand side. Neither was found necessary, and by 1917 were being removed, all being taken off as engines next went to works for repair.

There was a visible curiosity in the fixing of the cylinder block. The first two engines 2663 and 2664 (only) had two rows each of eight fixing bolts, which they kept through to withdrawal. The next seventy eight built had two rows each of only five bolts on each side, and widely spaced. They proved insufficient, and the last ten, built in 1915, had two rows each of nine. All except 2663/4 were quickly changed to that arrangement, but some of the early conversions from Precursor class, e.g. 2166 in January 1913, only had five bolts.

The coupled wheel bosses on the first twenty engines were of normal size, but from April 1911, large diameter boss became standard for the class. Because wheels were readily interchangeable, many examples could be seen of bosses differing from those first fitted. One of the last two to survive 25373, still had large bosses until late in its life, but by May 1947 had changed to the smaller type.

It was usual for the chimney to have a capuchon, and that was maintained through to withdrawal. The only deviation was noted on No.5000 where the upper portion had either corroded, or been turned off, but was restored subsequently. 25321, very late in LMS days, was changed to Stanier type chimney and from wheel to handle of the smokebox door.

2663 GEORGE THE FIFTH was experimental because it was superheated hence the fitting of pyrometer and mechanical lubricator. Leading sandbox has already been moved from below to above the running plate, but there is no rail on the cab yet. Note curve at edge of cab roof, and that it does not have Cooke sandshields.

The original fitting of Ramsbottom safety valves could still be seen around 1930. On the other hand, some acquired Ross pops whilst still in LNW livery, and all duly got that type. From 1924, replacement boilers had Belpaire instead of round-top firebox, and all that type had pops, which were also put on to some round-top fireboxes. Round-tops survived to the end of the class, 25373 keeping one, but the last Ramsbottom safety valves seem to have gone in the early 1930's. One engine only, No.2495 had a change of chimney position about 1915, when it was moved forward. That was to suit the fitting of an extra regulator on the superheater header at its outlet to the cylinders. The regulator in the dome was retained, but with operating rod outside instead of inside the boiler. That experiment ended during the 1914-18 war and 2495 became normal again. Unsuperheated engines had a displacement lubricator on each side of the smokebox for the valves and cylinders, but those with superheater had a mechanical lubricator mounted on the right hand frame. From the early 1920's, Beames had large oilboxes added, mounted on each handrail to serve driving journals.

One of Cooke's early additions was sandshields at the pipe outlets but few were fitted to this class. No.238 was noted with them, and that was in September 1914, before it was superheated but No.1792 also had them in its LNWR years. When new, all except the last ten had leading sandbox below the running plate behind the footstep. The 1915 builds had their boxes on the running plate, adjoining the splashers, and all the others were so altered.

Until 1933 all had taper shank buffers on circular base, but from then, when replacement was needed, Stanier type were fitted, which had parallel shank and square base. The LNW tried a Weir feed water heater, first on 127 and 2494 but by 1923 it was on 1472 which kept it until after it changed to 5371 but had lost it by August 1934.

Original tenders had one open coal rail, and were outwardly similar to those built for Precursors, but without toolboxes, which were replaced by cupboards. Coal space base was sloping instead of flat, to help coal move forward. Many changes of tender were made, this class getting both earlier, and later types, even including some of the R.O.D. type, although they were rather a rarity coupled to this class, at least five (5336, 5349, 5366, 5382 and 5402) are known to have been so equipped.

All except the last ten, built in 1915, got full LNWR painting, the 1915 batch lacking the lining due to the war, and the earlier ones followed suit, until lining could be restored in 1921. After Grouping they were to have red paint, lined in yellow, with small LMS on cab side, and 18" number on tender; by March 1924 seven 5329, 5365, 5377, 5393, 5394, 5403 and 5404 had that guise. Crewe then did little painting until 1926 but in April 1926 took plates off 1513 and 681, and put 6" high 5343 and 5390 in their place. During March to October 1927, five 5321, 5353, 5364 5366 and 5369 got red with armorial on cab, but from 1928 all went into black with 14" number on cab and LMS on tender. At the end of 1947 only three remained and 25321 went in February 1948. Although 25350 and 25373 were allocated B.R. numbers (58011 and 58012) both kept their LMS numbers, 25373 going early in May, and 25350 in w.e.22nd May 1948 which made the George the Fifth class extinct, sadly none being preserved.

2663 here in 1921 has been fitted to burn oil fuel, and probably has equipment transferred from 2585 WATT. It seems to be the only one of this class to be tried on oil firing. Pyrometer connection has been removed.

2663 at Willesden shed on 3rd June 1922 has had superheater damper removed. Note oil pipe from cab to smokebox, and at its base two rows each of eight bolts. Only 2663 and 2664 had eight, and both kept that number in contrast to all the others. *A.W.Croughton.*

GEORGE THE FIFTH CLASS

LNW No.	NAME	Built	LMS No.	Applied	To 2XXXX	With-drawn
2663	*GEORGE THE FIFTH*	7/10	5320	3/27	—	2/36
1059	*LORD LOCH*	11/10	5321	7/27	1/37	2/48
1294	*F.S.P.WOLFERSTAN*	11/10	5322	11/27	7/36	12/38
1583	*HENRY WARD*	11/10	5323	3/27	1/37	9/39
1725	*JOHN BATESON*	11/10	5324	3/28	2/37	11/38
2025	*SIR THOMAS BROOKE*	12/10	5325	12/27	2/26	5/37
2155	*W.C.BROCKLEHURST*	11/10	5326	6/27	6/36	12/36
228	*E.NETTLEFORD*	1/11	5327	1/27	—	9/36
445	*P.H.CHAMBRES*	1/11	5328	11/27	—	11/35
2664	*QUEEN MARY*	7/10	5329	2/24	—	3/36
1550	*WESTMINSTER*	10/10	5330	2/28	—	9/36
2271	*J.P.BICKERSTETH*	10/10	5331	7/27	8/36	11/38
896	*GEORGE WHALE*	10/10	5332	11/26	—	2/36
1559	*DRAKE*	10/10	5333	1/27	—	3/36
2151	*NEWCOMEN*	10/10	5334	9/26	2/37	11/37
2507	*MILES MAC INNES*	10/10	5335	12/27	—	11/35
238	*F.W.WEBB*	10/10	5336	3/28	—	3/36
1195	*T.J.HARE*	10/10	5337	8/26	—	7/36
2512	*THOMAS HOUGHTON*	10/10	5338	9/27	—	11/35
2168	*HENRY MAUDSLAY*	1/11	5339	12/27	9/36	4/37
956	*DACHSHUND (BULLDOG from 12/15)*	4/11	5340	12/27	—	11/35
1489	*WOLFHOUND*	4/11	5341	7/27	—	3/36
1504	*BOARHOUND*	4/11	5342	2/28	—	11/35
1513	*OTTERHOUND*	5/11	5343	4/26	—	4/36
1532	*BLOODHOUND*	5/11	5344	5/27	—	1/37
1628	*FOXHOUND*	5/11	5345	9/27	6/36	12/36
1662	*DEERHOUND*	5/11	5346	4/28	—	2/36
1706	*ELKHOUND*	5/11	5347	3/27	4/37	12/40
1800	*(for trials) then 5000 CORONATION*	6/11	5348	6/27	8/36	6/40
502	*BRITISH EMPIRE*	6/11	5349	12/26	—	7/36
868*	*INDIA (removed 9/36)*	6/11	5350	7/27	7/36	5/48
882	*CANADA*	6/11	5351	5/28	—	2/36
1218	*AUSTRALIA*	6/11	5352	5/26	—	11/35
1792	*STAGHOUND*	5/11	5353	9/27	—	6/36
2081	*NEW ZEALAND*	6/11	5354	12/26	---	1/36
2212	*SOUTH AFRICA*	6/11	5355	9/27	—	7/36
2291	*GIBRALTAR*	6/11	5356	11/27	9/36	8/41
2495	*BASSETHOUND*	5/11	5357	2/27	4/37	1/39
2177	*MALTA (removed 9/36)*	7/11	5358	10/27	—	11/36
2498	*CYPRUS (removed 9/36)*	7/11	5359	9/27	—	12/36
361	*BEAGLE*	7/11	5360	10/27	4/37	9/37
888	*CHALLENGER*	7/11	5361	3/27	—	11/35
1360	*FIRE QUEEN*	7/11	5362	8/27	4/37	3/39
1394	*HARRIER*	7/11	5363	9/27	—	2/36
1623	*NUBIAN*	8/11	5364	10/27	—	11/36
1631	*RACEHORSE*	8/11	5365	3/24	7/36	4/37
1644	*ROEBUCK*	8/11	5366	3/27	—	11/36
2089	*TRAVELLER*	8/11	5367	7/26	—	12/36
2494	*PERSEUS*	8/11	5368	9/27	4/34	11/36
1371	*QUAIL*	9/11	5369	6/27	5/36	9/36
1417	*LANDRAIL*	9/11	5370	12/27	—	12/36
1472	*MOOR HEN*	9/11	5371	7/27	8/36	10/39
1595	*WILD DUCK*	9/11	5372	9/27	6/36	12/36
1681**	*PTARMIGAN*	9/11	5373	5/26	5/36	5/48
2220	*VANGUARD*	8/11	5374	6/27	4/36	11/38
1713	*PARTRIDGE*	9/11	5375	11/27	—	12/35
1730	*SNIPE*	10/11	5376	7/27	10/36	12/47
1733	*GROUSE*	10/11	5377	11/23	8/36	7/37
1777	*WIDGEON*	10/11	5378	10/27	8/36	6/37
1799	*WOODCOCK*	10/11	5379	1/27	—	8/36
82	*CHARLES DICKENS*	1/13	5380	9/27	—	2/37
752	*JOHN HICK*	2/13	5381	12/27	—	11/35

LNW No.	NAME	Built	LMS No.	Applied	To 2XXXX	With-drawn
2124	*JOHN RENNIE*	2/13	5382	7/27	9/36	6/37
89	*JOHN MAYALL*	3/13	5383	11/27	—	5/36
132	*S.R.GRAVES*	3/13	5384	4/27	—	2/36
1138	*WILLIAM FROUDE*	2/13	5385	7/27	—	8/36
1193	*EDWARD TOOTAL*	3/13	5386	3/27	—	1/36
2154	*WILLIAM SIEMENS*	2/13	5387	6/27	6/36	2/37
2282	*RICHARD ARKWRIGHT*	2/13	5388	9/27	—	4/36
404	*ECLIPSE*	4/13	5389	9/27	5/36	6/37
681	*ST.GEORGE*	4/13	5390	4/26	—	11/35
845	*SADDLEBACK*	3/13	5391	1/27	—	2/36
1188	*PENMAENMAWR*	4/13	5392	2/28	8/36	2/41
1680	*LOYALTY*	4/13	5393	2/24	3/36	5/41
2086	*PHAETON*	4/13	5394	2/24	—	7/36
2279	*HENRY CROSFIELD*	3/13	5395	6/27	—	2/37
1481	*TYPHON*	4/13	5396	6/28	—	10/36
2197	*PLANET (removed 8/33)*	4/13	5397	3/28	—	12/35
2242	*METEOR (removed 8/33)*	5/13	5398	7/27	—	10/36
2428	*LORD STALBRIDGE*	5/13	5399	9/27	—	7/36
363	*LLANDUDNO*	5/15	5400	8/27	—	11/35
789	*WINDERMERE*	5/15	5401	6/27	—	2/36
984	*CARNARAVON*	5/15	5402	2/27	—	6/36
104	*LEAMINGTON (SPA added 12/15)*	6/15	5403	2/24	—	11/35
226	*COLWYN BAY*	6/15	5404	10/23	—	2/36
1086	*CONWAY*	6/15	5405	2/28	—	1/36
2153	*LLANDRINDOD*	6/15	5406	6/26	—	4/37
2233	*BLACKPOOL*	6/15	5407	12/27	—	11/35
2106	*HOLYHEAD*	7/15	5408	9/27	—	5/37
2370	*DOVEDALE*	7/15	5409	9/26	6/37	6/39

* *Allocated BR 58011 in March 1948 but not applied.*
** *Allocated BR 58012 in March 1948 but not applied.*

2664 QUEEN MARY was superheated from June 1913, and had damper gear fitted, but it kept two rows of eight bolts. Sandbox has been moved but it still has original tender type introduced for this class. *Real Photos.*

228 E.NETTLEFOLD as built in January 1911 was one of the nine superheated engines like 2663, but having two rows of only five bolts. Note original position of front sandbox below running plate behind footstep, and new design of tender with a single open coal rail, and cupboards instead of tool boxes.

2106 HOLYHEAD was one of the final ten, built May-July 1917 which had two rows of nine bolts when built, also damper gear, sandbox on running plate, but no rail on cab. War conditions caused these ten to have black paint but no lining or armorial. *National Railway Museum.*

1550 WESTMINSTER was not superheated until September 1913 when it was changed at base of smokebox from two rows of five to two rows of nine bolts. Sandbox has been moved to above running plate, but it does not have sandshields. Outlet for pyrometer was provided but no connecting pipe to cab. *LNWR Society.*

5367 TRAVELLER so numbered in July 1926 had these 10" figures put on in place of its cast plates, but kept LNW lining. Boiler is original type with two washout plugs, round top firebox, and Ramsbottom safety valves. *A.G.Ellis.*

1800 (without name) was one of the first production batch, begun in April 1911 after deciding in favour of superheating as standard, so it has pyrometer and mechanical lubricator, but sandbox still below running plate. All seventy built from April 1911 had large boss in their coupled wheels. 1800 only ran trial trips with that number. *A.G.Ellis.*

(above) **5000 CORONATION was 1800 changed and named for George V's crowning in June 1911 when this engine entered traffic. The engine continued to carry its works number as its running number to June 1927 when it became LMS 5348. Here at Manchester, its front sandbox has been moved above running plate, pyrometer is still fitted, but rail has not yet been put on to cab.**

25373 PTARMIGAN here after May 1936, still has one of the original boilers with two plugs, but has had Ross pop safety valves put on a Ramsbottom mounting.

2291 GIBRALTAR, at Camden shed, got this Belpaire firebox boiler in June 1925 but kept LNW number until November 1927. These replacement boilers had their own mounting for the Ross pop safety valves. Note addition of Beames oil box mounted on the boiler handrail. *LPC.*

25373 here at Crewe Works on 31st May 1947 has had its coupled wheels changed to those with small boss as fitted to the first twenty of the class built to January 1911. Rear edge of the cab roof still has the holder for the LNW type shed plate. *H.C.Casserley*

5339 HENRY MAUDSLAY has been changed to wheels with large boss which have crescent shaped balance weight in the driving pair, and all spokes flared to the rim. Lamp sockets have been superseded by irons. *Real Photos.*

5334 NEWCOMEN was one of at least twenty (5356, 5358, 5359, 5364, 5367, 5371, 5392, 5396, 5408, 5409, 25321, 25322, 25345, 25347, 25357, 25367, 25371, 25373 and 25393) which, from the mid-1930's, were fitted with LMS buffers which had square flange and parallel shank. The LMS shed plate 3D shows its allocation was Aston. *Photomatic.*

5390 ST. GEORGE was given its LMS number in April 1926 in 6" painted figures, where LNW numberplate has been removed.

1472 MOOR HEN was fitted pre1917 with Weir feed water heating apparatus as here with LNW lining. Note cab cross rail not yet fitted. *Real Photos.*

5327 E.NETTLEFOLD here at Rugby in 1934 has had LNW shed plate moved forward and this No.2 indicates Willesden, later 1A. Note that when altered to MR gauge, a curved rain strip replaced the original straight type.
W.L.Good.

5364 NUBIAN, so numbered in October 1927, from LNW 1623, later got red painting with yellow lining panels on cab, but was paired with an un-lined black tender. Here in July 1935 it is at Chester.

5404 COLWYN BAY had been LNW 226 until it got its LMS number in October 1923 and this red painting with yellow lining. The cab lettering was intended to be temporary until transfers for the emblem became available. A cast plate on smokebox door shows engine number, repeated on the tender in 18" figures.

5408 HOLYHEAD had a numberplate put on the smokebox door in September 1927, but when cab numbering became standard, those plates usually were removed, as on this one. Note it is now fitted with Stanier type buffers, which were introduced in 1933.

Beginning in February 1936, it was desired to clear the 5320-5409 number range to allow new Stanier 'Black Fives' to have those numbers. Surviving 'Georges' thus had their numbers increased by 20000. When done by a shed, that put the number off-centre as seen on 25376 SNIPE at Chester.
N.E.Preedy Collection.

25348 had number increased in August 1936, and in keeping with its special nameplate, it was done properly by the Works. In 1992 at an auction in Sheffield, one of these plates was sold for £21,000.
W.L.Good.

25392 however survived to have that number applied properly in August 1936, and then continued in service until February 1941. *L.W.Perkins.*

5391 SADDLEBACK here at Crewe North shed in May 1935 has one of the 1905 design of tender which had two open coal rails, and had been built for Precursor or Experiment class.

5335 MILES MAC INNES at Rugby on 3rd June 1934 has the 1916 design tender, with stronger frame, square rear end, and altered shape of frame slots. It was introduced on Claughtons built from July 1916.

5336 F.W.WEBB at Rugby on 3rd June 1934 has been paired with one of the tenders bought cheaply from the Railway Operating Division .

5000 CORONATION taking water from Whitmore troughs is on a Birmingham to Liverpool express, a typical duty for which the class was built. Note that, most unusually, the chimney has no capuchon.
Real Photos.

1218 AUSTRALIA at Kenton, shows that although built for main line express passenger work, they were also put to work other revenue producing trains. Despite hauling a fully loaded 40 wagon goods train, 1218 has steam to spare.
Real Photos.

5365 RACEHORSE in LMS red painting sometime in 1924 is at Kenton with an express for Euston.

(above) **5377 GROUSE with LNW 27 (Preston) shed plate, is assisting exL&Y 4-6-0 No.10408 to climb Grayrigg bank with a Birmingham-Glasgow express of at least 14 coaches, in 1934.**

5371 MOOR HEN is leaving Crewe with an up main line express after removal of the feed water heating apparatus in 1928. Note that it has been fitted with smokebox number plate from July 1927. *N.E Preedy Collection.*

25334 NEWCOMEN in October 1937 with LMS type shedplate 2B for Nuneaton, is leaving Cambridge with a class B goods train. *R.F.Roberts.*

5340 BULLDOG changed to that name from the original DACHSHUND in December 1915 to remove the German connection. As LNW 956 it was the first of the class to be fitted with the large bosses to coupled wheels. Here on the dump at Rugby on 14th September 1935, it had been set aside at the end of the summer traffic, and it was withdrawn in the following November. *W.L.Good*

25321 LORD LOCH finally ran fitted with this Stanier design chimney. The wheel for fastening the smokebox door was replaced by a second handle. It was the only one of the class so altered. That alteration began about 1944. *W.L.Good.*

1792 STAGHOUND is still fitted with a superheater damper control and with sandshields for all coupled wheels in this pre-1917 photograph, and it still has its leading sand boxes below the running plate.

5382 JOHN RENNIE with R.O.D. tender, Edge Hill shed July 24th 1932. *W.L.Good.*

5366 ROEBUCK changed to its LMS number in March 1927 and was one of the few to be painted red and get LMS armorial on the cab. In 1927 it was rare for lamp sockets to be retained and not have them changed to irons. An R.O.D. tender is also attached.

Although the negative is damaged, it is worth including this view of 5355 SOUTH AFRICA to show the single yellow lining on what is believed to black and not red livery.

5376 had the 2 prefix added in October 1936 and as it was done by a shed the result was off centre. In that guise it had a Belpaire firebox boiler. When next "shopped" it reverted to a round-top firebox and the number was centred and applied in back-shaded figures, as seen here. The tender is a 1916 design to which rails have been added to keep the fire irons secure.

W.Potter.

WHALE'S "EXPERIMENT" CLASS 4-6-0 PASSENGER ENGINES

This class was a direct development of Whale's successful Precursor design, having the additional adhesion of an extra pair of coupled wheels, which were also 6" smaller in diameter. The main purpose was to enable them to deal with heavier trains, especially on the Crewe to Carlisle line. The LNWR made only one major alteration, and limited that to a single engine, just for experimental trial. In March 1915, No.1361 was rebuilt to a 4-cylinder simple with Dendy-Marshall valve gear, and fitted with a Schmidt superheater. When renumbered by the LMS it was put at the end of the class as 5554, instead of in date of order of building, and it remained as rebuilt until its June 1933 withdrawal.

Only two others of this class were fitted with superheater, 2624 (which kept that LNW number) from February 1926 to its withdrawal in February 1928, and 1993 which changed to 5472 when it was superheated in December 1926, but that one lost its superheater in a January 1932 repair. Neither showed any outward evidence of being superheated, because their smokebox was not extended, nor was a snifter, or mechanical lubrication fitted.

Original chimneys did not have a capuchon fitted, but quite a number had one added later, although it never became a standard fitting for this class. Boilers to replace those first fitted, and designed by Beames, began to be fitted in 1924, and had Belpaire type firebox carrying pop type safety valves, and at least 24 were recorded as so changed. Photographs confirm numbers 2624, 5450, 5469, 25473, 5479, 5484, 5488, 5525, 5526, 25528, and 5548, whilst 5451, 5456, 5457, 5458, 5461, 5462, 5467, 5474, 5476, 5482, 5513, 5534 and 5539 are on record as so fitted. Safety valves were also changed from Ramsbottom to pops on many of the round-top firebox boilers, pops having become standard in 1920. The original boiler design had only two washout plugs on each side, increased to four on replacements, and there were four on all the Belpaires.

All except possibly the eleven (5455, 5465, 5481, 5486, 5493, 5503, 5515, 5517, 5527, 5538, 5544) which were withdrawn in June to October 1925, were fitted with the extra oilboxes mounted on each boiler handrail, and having five vertical feed pipes down to the coupled wheel bearings, which Beames introduced in early LMS years.

By the time that they changed from LNW to LMS numbering, most had also been altered from the LNW socket lampholders to LMS lamp irons, but 5450 and 5516 still had sockets after they got LMS numbers. Little variation of buffer type was seen. When new they had the Whale short taper-shank type, but many were changed to the Cooke 3" longer taper-shank type.

Odd details tried, but soon discarded, were plates at the front of the bogie to protect from water thrown up by a pilot engine when picking up from track troughs. Only 353 and 1020 were noted so fitted about 1918/19. Strangely, for main line passenger engines, very few had Cooke's sandshields fitted, again only two, 2638 in July 1921, and 1709 in June 1922 were so observed.

After Grouping, many had their cab roof modified to enable them to comply with the slightly more restrictive Midland loading gauge. The height from rail had to be reduced, particularly at the sides, the LNW flattening of the curve having to be discarded. Along with that alteration, a curved rain strip was fitted. All those which got Belpaire firebox had that cab roof alteration.

The whole class originally had the same type of tender as introduced for the Precursor class, which had two open rails, and a tool box at the front end on each side. There were some subsequent changes of tender type, amongst which the 1916 Cooke final LNW design, and even purchased R.O.D. were included.

Experiment class was never accorded LMS red painting, nor did any get small LMS in a panel on the cab side, because all kept their LNW numbering until April 1926. In that month 5469, 5473, 5501 and 5510 had their LNW numberplates taken off, and those LMS numbers painted only 6" high in their place. Then, to the end of 1927, the circular armorial was put on the cab side, and the number in 18" figures on the tender. Engines repainted later got 14" number on cab side with matching height LMS on the tender. In mid-1934, the thirteen which still survived had their numbers increased by 20,000 to avoid duplication with new 4-6-0 engines of Stanier design, but Experiment class was extinct when 25473 was the last to be withdrawn in September 1935.

66's official photograph, as built; note no capuchon on chimney, no sanding to middle coupled wheels, no cross rail on cab, all which were added later. Tender is same type as built for Precursor class.

EXPERIMENT CLASS 4-6-0 PASSENGER ENGINES

LNW No.	NAME	Built	LMS No.	Applied	To 2XXXX	With-drawn
66	*EXPERIMENT*	4/05	5450	6/26	—	7/31
306	*AUTOCRAT*	7/05	5451	7/27	—	12/30
353	*BRITANNIC*	6/05	5452	2/27	—	12/30
372	*GERMANIC (BELGIC from 10/14)*	6/05	5453	11/26	—	9/28
507	*SARMATIAN*	6/05	5454	6/26	—	9/32
565	*CITY OF CARLISLE*	1/06	(5455)	——	—	6/25
893	*CITY OF CHESTER*	1/06	5456	2/28	4/34	8/35
1074	*CITY OF DUBLIN*	1/06	5457	2/28	—	9/34
1357	*CITY OF EDINBURGH*	1/06	5458	8/27	—	12/33
165	*CITY OF LICHFIELD*	1/06	5459	6/26	—	12/30
828	*CITY OF LIVERPOOL*	2/06	5460	5/27	—	10/34
978	*CITY OF LONDON*	2/06	5461	9/27	—	5/34
1405	*CITY OF MANCHESTER*	2/06	5462	5/26	—	11/34
1575	*CITY OF PARIS*	2/06	5463	7/27	—	9/28
1669	*CITY OF GLASGOW*	1/06	5464	9/26	—	12/30
1986	*CLANRICARDE*	9/06	(5465)	——	—	10/25
1987	*GLENDOWER*	9/06	5466	6/26	—	11/34
1988	*HURRICANE*	9/06	5467	2/27	—	9/28
1989	*LADY OF THE LAKE (removed 12/28)*	9/06	5468	4/27	—	12/29
1990	*NORTH WESTERN*	10/06	5469	4/26	—	3/32
1991	*PALMERSTON*	10/06	5470	6/27	—	2/28
1992	*PRESIDENT*	10/06	5471	8/26	—	12/33
1993	*RICHARD MOON (superheated 12/26 to 1/32)*	10/06	5472	12/26	—	12/33
1994	*SCOTTISH CHIEF*	10/06	5473	4/26	6/34	9/35
61	*ATALANTA*	11/06	5474	11/27	—	12/33
222	*IVANHOE*	11/06	5475	6/27	—	7/35
291	*LEANDER*	11/06	5476	9/27	—	9/31
667	*MAZEPPA*	11/06	5477	4/27	—	12/33
1304	*PROMETHEUS*	11/06	5478	3/27	—	8/31
1676	*PRINCE OF WALES (SHAKESPEARE from 7/11)*	11/06	5479	9/27	—	11/34
1709	*PRINCESS MAY*	11/06	5480	4/27	—	2/28
1995	*TORNADO*	10/06	(5481)	——	—	9/25
2027	*QUEEN EMPRESS*	11/06	5482	1/28	—	10/31
2052	*STEPHENSON*	12/06	5483	8/26	—	12/30
2269	*WILLIAM CAWKWELL*	12/06	5484	8/26	—	8/31
496	*HARLEQUIN*	9/07	5485	11/26	—	8/30
830	*PHOSPHORUS*	9/07	(5486)	——	—	7/25
902	*COMBERMERE*	9/07	5487	2/27	—	10/34
937	*PRINCESS ALICE*	9/07	5488	7/26	—	3/34
1014	*HENRY BESSEMER*	9/07	5489	10/26	—	3/28
2112	*VICTORIA*	9/07	5490	2/27	—	12/30
1135	*PRINCE GEORGE*	9/07	5491	3/27	—	6/34
1526	*SANSPAREIL*	10/07	5492	11/26	—	11/28
2161	*JEANIE DEANS*	10/07	(5493)	——	—	8/25
322	*ADRIATIC*	12/08	5494	6/27	—	6/29
884	*GREATER BRITAIN*	12/08	5495	1/28	—	12/30
887	*FORTUNA*	1/09	5496	1/28	—	3/32
1020	*MAJESTIC*	1/09	5497	9/27	—	11/34
1483	*RED GAUNTLET*	1/09	5498	6/27	—	12/33
1490	*WELLINGTON*	1/09	5499	12/27	—	12/33
1553	*FARADAY*	1/09	5500	6/27	—	10/31
1571	*HERSCHEL*	1/09	5501	4/26	—	1/29
2076	*PHEASANT*	1/09	5502	12/26	4/34	10/34
2116	*GREYSTOKE*	1/09	(5503)	——	—	7/25
2621	*ETHELRED*	2/09	5504	5/27	4/34	11/34
2622	*EUNOMIA*	2/09	5505	8/26	—	4/28
2623	*LORD OF THE ISLES*	2/09	5506	10/26	—	3/34
2624	*SARACEN (superheated from 2/26)*	2/09	(5507)	——	—	2/28
2625	*BUCKLAND*	2/09	5508	5/27	4/34	8/35
2626	*CHILLINGTON*	2/09	5509	2/27	4/34	5/35
2627	*PRESIDENT LINCOLN*	2/09	5510	4/26	—	5/28
2628	*BANSHEE*	2/09	5511	8/27	4/34	7/35

LNW No.	NAME	Built	LMS No.	Applied	To 2XXXX	With-drawn
2629	*TERRIER*	3/09	5512	7/26	---	2/28
2630	*BUFFALO*	3/09	5513	7/27	---	3/32
1406	*GEORGE FINDLAY*	4/09	5514	6/27	4/34	8/35
1413	*HENRY CORT*	4/09	(5515)	——	—	9/25
1477	*HUGH MYDDLETON*	5/09	5516	7/26	—	4/28
1498	*THOMAS SAVERY*	5/09	(5517)	——	—	9/25
1566	*JOHN PENN*	5/09	5518	11/26	—	12/33
1603	*PRINCESS ALEXANDRA*	5/09	5519	3/27	—	12/30
1649	*SISYPHUS*	5/09	5520	6/27	—	9/32
1661	*WORDSWORTH*	5/09	5521	12/26	—	6/28
1781	*LIGHTNING*	5/09	5522	7/27	—	5/30
2022	*MARLBOROUGH*	5/09	5523	6/27	—	4/34
2637	*BABYLON*	6/09	5524	2/27	—	1/32
2638	*BYZANTIUM*	6/09	5525	2/27	3/34	6/34
2639	*BACTRIA*	6/09	5526	6/27	—	4/34
2640	*BELISARIUS*	6/09	(5527)	——	—	9/25
2641	*BELLONA*	6/09	5528	1/28	4/34	8/35
2642	*BERENICE*	6/09	5529	9/27	—	12/33
2643	*BACCHUS*	6/09	(5530)	——	—	10/27
2644	*BERENGARIA*	6/09	5531	7/26	5/34	8/34
2645	*BRITOMART*	7/09	5532	6/27	5/34	9/34
2646	*BONIFACE*	7/09	5533	2/27	—	9/28
1412	*BEDFORDSHIRE*	11/09	5534	10/27	—	1/32
1418	*CHESHIRE*	11/09	5535	2/27	—	12/31
1420	*DERBYSHIRE*	11/09	5536	6/27	—	12/33
1455	*HEREFORDSHIRE*	11/09	5537	7/27	—	12/33
1611	*HERTFORDSHIRE*	11/09	(5538)	——	—	9/25
1618	*LANCASHIRE*	11/09	5539	1/28	—	3/34
71	*OXFORDSHIRE*	12/09	5540	9/26	—	4/28
275	*SHROPSHIRE*	12/09	5541	10/26	—	9/28
677	*STAFFORDSHIRE*	12/09	5542	8/27	—	12/33
1002	*WARWICKSHIRE*	12/09	5543	6/27	—	12/30
1534	*WESTMORLAND*	12/09	(5544)	——	—	9/25
1624	*LEICESTERSHIRE*	11/09	5545	6/26	—	12/33
1652	*MIDDLESEX*	11/09	5546	8/27	—	12/33
1689	*MONMOUTHSHIRE*	12/09	5547	6/26	—	3/32
1703	*NORTHUMBERLAND*	12/09	5548	6/26	—	3/34
1471	*WORCESTERSHIRE*	1/10	5549	7/27	—	3/32
1561	*YORKSHIRE*	1/10	5550	10/26	—	9/28
1618	*CARNARVONSHIRE*	1/10	5551	12/27	—	3/34
1621	*DENBIGHSHIRE*	1/10	5552	7/27	4/34	6/35
1658	*FLINTSHIRE*	1/10	5553	4/27	—	7/31
1361	*PROSPERO (rebuilt 3/15 to 4-cylinders)*	10/07	5554	2/27	—	6/33

2027 QUEEN EMPRESS shows that first changes were removal of the lubricator from base of smokebox, and addition of sanding to the middle coupled wheels from boxes placed inside the splashers. *A.G.Ellis.*

165 CITY OF LICHFIELD shows early changes were removal of lubricator from smokebox side, fitting of capuchon on chimney, and a handrail across the side of the cab.

PROSPERO was rebuilt in March 1915 to 4-cylinders, Dendy Marshall valve gear, and fitted with a Schmidt superheater. When the L M S renumbered 1361, instead of the expected 5492 according to date of building, its singularity was recognised by making it 5554, the last one in the Experiment 5450-5554 range. *N.E.Preedy Collection.*

2624 SARACEN had a superheater fitted in February 1926 when it got Belpaire firebox, but was not renumbered, and still had LNW number when withdrawn in February 1928. No snifters, extended smokebox, or mechanical lubricator were put on, but there was extra lubrication from cab. Note square end balance weight over three spokes of leading wheel.

66 EXPERIMENT here still has original type boiler, with Ramsbottom safety valves, and two washout plugs. Beames oilbox has been added, also sandbox inside splasher to serve middle coupled wheels.

5500 FARADAY has original type boiler, but Ross pop safety valves have been put on to the mounting which had the Ramsbottom type. Lamp irons have also replaced the sockets. *Real Photos.*

5526 BACTRIA with Belpaire firebox has been cut down to pass the Midland load gauge. Note slightly shorter chimney, also middle and rear wheel balancing. At Crewe South 15th April 1934 it has just been withdrawn. *W.L.Good.*

1561 YORKSHIRE has the shorter length Whale buffers extended with packing pieces to match the different screw coupling. Here, as built, the chimney has no capuchon fitted, but tender type has changed.

372 BELGIC has the longer Cooke buffers, and is seen after its renaming in October 1914. Note there is no handrail fitted across the side of the cab, and sanding to middle coupled wheels has yet to be added.
Real Photos.

1020 MAJESTIC has been fitted experimentally with dust shields on the bogie to protect from anything thrown up by a pilot engine. 353 BRITANNIC in June 1919 was the only other Experiment seen so fitted. This up goods is at Bletchley in 1918, and shields were soon taken off.
F.W.Goslin per The Gresley Society.

5472 RICHARD MOON was the only one of the class noted as changed to one of the second-hand tenders bought from the Government's Railway Operating Division.

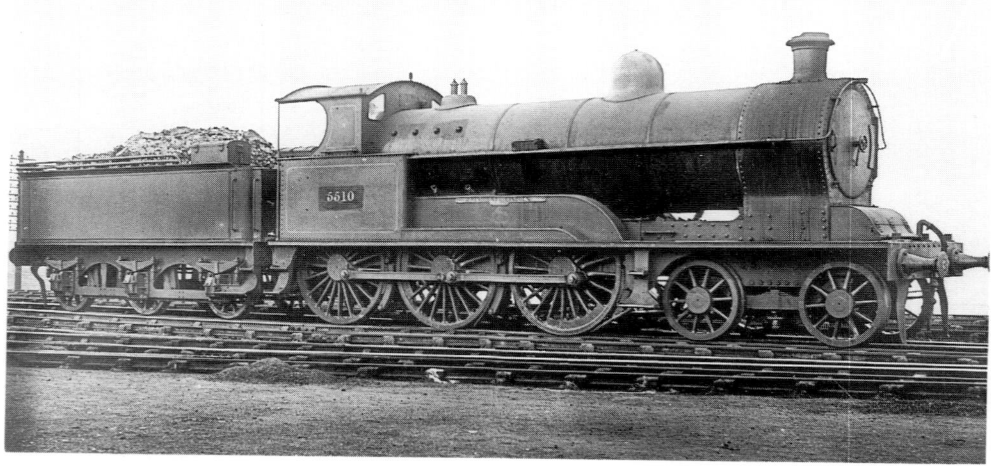

5469, 5473, 5501, 5510 in April, and 5462 in May 1926 were the first of the class changed from LNW to LMS number, and 5510 just had that number painted in small figures on the space vacated by the LNW 2627 plate. It kept LNW lining, and did not get Midland style cast number plate put on smokebox door.

5450 EXPERIMENT was one of seven (5454, 5459, 5466, 5545, 5547, 5548 also) to be renumbered in June 1926. It, and at least 5548, got Midland style numberplate fitted on smokebox door. Cab had circular emblem put on, but painting was plain black, and without number on tender.

5513 BUFFALO was a July 1927 renumbering, and was treated the same as 5450, except that number in 18" figures was put on the tender. 5488 also renumbered in July 1927 was done in the same style as 5513. *A.G.Ellis.*

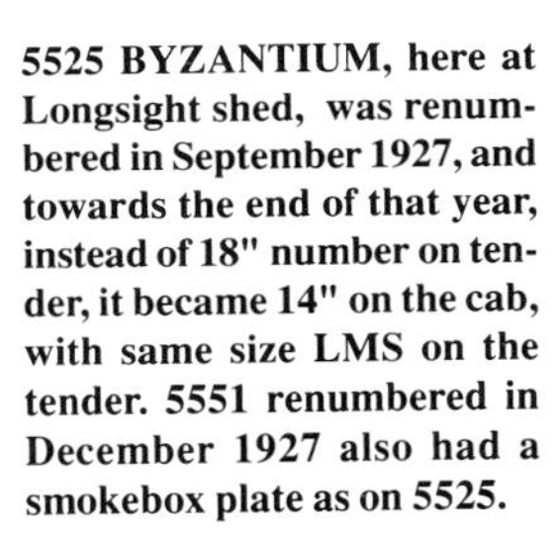

5525 BYZANTIUM, here at Longsight shed, was renumbered in September 1927, and towards the end of that year, instead of 18" number on tender, it became 14" on the cab, with same size LMS on the tender. 5551 renumbered in December 1927 also had a smokebox plate as on 5525.

5504 ETHELRED, so renumbered in May 1927 would be fitted with smokebox plate, but here, with number on cab, shows no evidence of having one. Note the customary LMS is missing on tender.

1412 BEDFORDSHIRE at Bushey shows the kind of heavy express work this class did in their early years. Displacement lubricator has not yet been taken off, but tender has changed to George V type.

(left) **372 originally named GERMANIC was changed in October 1914 to BELGIC due to public outrage at Germany's callous invasion of Belgium. To add emphasis to the odium generally felt, the original name was retained but scored through, and a new plate put above it.**

(below) **2643 BACCHUS is piloting 561 ANTAEUS on the troughs at Dillicar with an Edinburgh - Euston express; 2643 is in original condition, and before capuchon was fitted.**

5553 FLINTSHIRE was the last of the class built, and here at Tebay is assisting a Hughes 2-6-0 on an up class B goods. Renumbered in April 1927 it got smokebox plate, and cab number in 1929, but was withdrawn in July 1931.

By September 1926 when CITY OF GLASGOW changed from LNW 1669 to LMS 5464 it was already twenty years old, so it is no surprise to see it demoted to working a No.1 express milk or fruit train. Shedded at Bletchley, it has lamp irons instead of sockets, and pops instead of Ramsbottom safety valves, but still has original type tender.

As the class multiplied, they were able to take on work other than that of the Crewe to Carlisle main line for which they were built. 2626 CHILLINGTON is at Stalybridge working a Manchester-Huddersfield-Leeds stopping train. Displacement lubricator has gone from smokebox side, capuchon has not yet been fitted on chimney, but a horizontal hand rail has been put on the cab side.

5461 CITY OF LONDON here on 26th March 1933, is leaving Northampton (Castle) with an express. It was withdrawn in May 1934 and did not have the 2XXXX addition to its number. *L.Hanson.*

25509 CHILLINGTON had number increased in April 1934 and applied properly. Here on 8th July 1934 it is leaving Northampton (Castle)It was withdrawn in May 1935, when only seven others remained. *L.Hanson.*

5546 MIDDLESEX at Crewe shows the filler of the sandbox for the middle coupled wheels, which was added inside the splasher.

NORTH WESTERN happened to be one of those in Crewe Works in April 1926 when they were adjured to speed up their application of LMS numbers, so its LNW 1990 plates were taken off and 5469 in six inch numerals was painted in their place. Here at Peterborough shed on 17th May 1927 it had not then had lamp irons fitted in place of sockets. *H.C.Casserley.*

On LNW 1483 there was no doubt about the name RED GAUNTLET being two words, unlike on the similarly named one on the North British which had it as a single one. Because 1483 has had Beames oil boxes fitted, this photograph at Tamworth (Low Level) is 1921 or later. *Lens of Sutton.*

5488 PRINCESS ALICE got that number in July 1926, with plate fitted on smokebox door, eighteen inch figures on the tender and armorial on the cab, but all on unlined black painting.

5487 COMBERMERE is approaching Tamworth with a down local passenger train on 4th June 1927, having acquired smokebox plate and armorial on the cab in the previous February, when probably the lamp irons replaced sockets. *W.L.Good.*

25531 BERENGARIA has clearly had the extra 2 added to its number at a shed, causing this 'off-centre' result. That number alteration only began in mid-1934 and 25531 was withdrawn in August, so a photographic record of it is fortunate.

5479 SHAKESPEARE at Crewe on 13th October 1935, bereft of shed plate and tender, needed the CONDEMNED indication because it had been withdrawn in November 1934. From new in November 1906 to July 1911 its name was PRINCE OF WALES - the one who became George V. That name was then used on 819, the first of a new class, and that P.of W. became Edward VIII. *W.L.Good.*

COOKE "PRINCE OF WALES" 4-6-0 PASSENGER ENGINES

The unusual conditions caused by the 1914-18 war made Crewe Works depart from its tradition of building all the engines required by the LNWR. The 245 engines of the class introduced from October 1911 included twenty built October 1915 to January 1916 by North British Locomotive Co., and another ninety by William Beardmore & Co., also in Glasgow, from June 1921 to April 1922, Crewe building the other 135. Those from the contractors could be recognised in LNW days because they had maker's works plate on each side of their smokebox, North British being circular, and Beardmore rectangular. None of these plates survived the change from LNW to LMS numbering done in 1923 to 1928.

This design was essentially a stretched version of Cooke's George the Fifth class, other differences being minimal. The bogie wheels were 3' 9" instead of 3' 3", the coupled wheels were 6' 3" as against 6' 9", and did not have the large circular bosses as on the 4-4-0 type. At the base of the smokebox on each side a snifting valve was fitted, and on the front plate were oil boxes serving the piston tail rods, clearly visible because no curved cover plate was fitted as on the 4-4-0 engines. The tender differed by having springs with straight tops, and its side sheets had a solid top with double beading, instead of coal rails.

In 1911, experience with superheating was limited, so the first forty engines had a pyrometer fitted on the right hand side, and on the other side was operating gear for a damper. Neither proved essential so, from about 1916, were normally removed, but LNW No.940 built in 1919 still had damper operating gear when seen in 1928, and LMS 5827 still had pyrometer connection after it had that number moved to its cab in March 1928. It was customary for the chimney to carry a capuchon, and very rarely were any seen with a plain top, although No.1089 was without capuchon when seen in 1920.

All began with normal smokebox door fastened by wheel and handle, augmented by four dog clips. In the early 1930's, a door fastened only by eight dog clips began to be used on the class, those so noted being 5640 (16.7.33), 5659 (2.4.32), 25608 (3.3.35), 25681 (14.4.35), 25691 (14.9.35) and 25788 (2.8.36). That type door also had the top lamp iron fitted on it, and although of smaller diameter, was the style that had been introduced in 1928 when the larger diameter boiler was put on to Claughton class. On those with normal door which survived in 1944/45, the wheel was replaced by a handle.

Whilst still in LNWR ownership, Beames had designed a revised boiler for this class with Belpaire, instead of round-top firebox, and with pop safety valves instead of Ramsbottom type; those boilers began to be fitted in 1924. During the 1920's some of the original boilers had pops put on to existing Ramsbottom mountings.

All were first fitted with buffers of Cooke's long taper-shank type which had a circular flange, but from 1933, any replacements needed were of Stanier design, which had parallel shank and a square flange.

The ninety engines built to April 1916 (70 by Crewe and 20 by N.B.Loco. Co.) were all named, and their leading sandboxes were below the running plate, where they remained. On those built sub-

The first of the class in LMS days, painted red and lined, as LMS 5600 from October 1924. *Real Photos.*

819 PRINCE OF WALES was the first of forty built by Crewe from October 1911 to March 1914, all named, and fully lined. As superheated, they had long smokebox, pyrometer and mechanical lubricator on the right hand side, and snifter at base of smokebox. 819 here at Stockport still has a tender of the 1910 design with a single open coal rail, as fitted only to the first ten. *A.G.Ellis.*

sequently, the sandboxes were mounted on the running plate adjoining the front of the splasher. The sixty five which Crewe built in 1919 were not then given names, but in 1922, twelve (only) acquired nameplates. None of the ninety built by Beardmore for the LNW were ever named, but they did have one significant difference of detail. Instead of the traditional sockets for the lamps, they had irons, to which the LMS changed the earlier engines.

On 9th August 1923, an order was issued for ten Prince of Wales class to have cab roof altered to comply with the Midland loading gauge; No.1321, then 812 and 1341 were the first to be done, all in August 1923. Many subsequently got this modification, mainly from 1928 to 1934, as did all those with Belpaire firebox.

In 1921 Beames began an alteration to the lubrication of the coupled wheel bearings. A large oil box was mounted on the boiler handrail at each side, both having five feed pipes down to the journals. All duly acquired them, although after changing to LMS livery in March 1924, 5839 was still without, and so was No.5829 in 1926 when fitted for oil fuel firing. During the 1926 coal strike, at least forty five of this class were adapted to burn oil fuel. There was variation as to how it was carried on the tender; 5607, 5630, 5661 and 5829 had two large cylindrical tanks, but 5651 and 5671 only had a single rectangular tank.

No less than five types of tender could be seen coupled to engines of this class. The prototype No.819 had tender differing from earlier designs at the top of its side sheets, having a solid top with double beading instead of coal rails. Tenders of 1905 design with two open coal rails, and those of 1910 design with a single open coal rail were coupled with Princes when convenient. The final LNWR tender design was built from 1916, and that had a solid coping and a single beading, but it had noticeably different frames from all those built from 1905. The frame was both longer and stronger, with main slots parallel top and bottom, joined by semicircular ends, and many superseded earlier tender types on this class. Use was also made of tenders from ex-R.O.D. engines; they

964 BRET HARTE built February 1914 and here at Manchester (London Road) in 1916, still has all the original features of the first forty. Boiler has two washout plugs, Ramsbottom safety valves, and damper operating gear. Only the first forty had oil boxes at front for the piston tail rods and they were removed about 1916. Leading sandbox is below running plate with middle one inside the splasher, and leading pipe has Cooke sandshield. Tender has double beaded solid coping, introduced for this class. Note snifting valve at base of smokebox.

had deep, stepped-out copings of solid plate, and were of Great Central Railway design.
It is believed that the first ninety engines originally had full LNWR lining, but the remaining 155 were definitely plain black when new. Lined engines repainted in 1916-21 also went into plain black, but from October 1921 lining was resumed.
The LMS accorded red livery to this class 5791, 5809 and 5843, all in September 1923, are believed to have been the first Princes to receive it. The new number was on the tender in 18" figures, and on the cab panel LMS in 4½" letters took the place of the LNW cast brass number plate. By March 1924, eight others, 5662, 5668, 5729, 5738, 5770, 5788, 5807 and 5838 are known to have been done in that style. By June 1924 when 5839 was painted red, the circular emblem was being used instead of the small letters. The large-scale re-organisation of Crewe Works precluded normal painting until during 1926, but just over 20 were recorded in red paint. Crewe's long established custom of switching tenders - hitherto perfectly easy with tenders having plain sides - quickly led to difficulty when an engine number was prominently displayed on them. An effort in 1924 to resolve this was made on 5788, which was given numbering on four separate detachable plates, (similar to those on cricket scoreboards) for altering numbers when needed. That idea was found impractical under working conditions, so was discarded. In April 1926 Crewe were exhorted to speed up the change to LMS numbering, and on engines then in for repair they just removed the LNW cast plate and simply painted the new number in 6" figures on the space vacated. Three of those so done were simultaneously changed to firing by oil fuel. From the end of 1927 it was decided to put the engine number in 14" figures on the cab but on some it was first applied in 10" as on 5644 and 5690. In December 1928 it was decided that this class should be painted black, relieved only by single red lining. Even so, exceptions took place, because in 1935, two of the class, 25673 and 25732 got red paint and single yellow lining
All 245 duly changed to LMS numbering 5600 to 5844, the last to do so being 5820 (ex LNW 354) in September 1928. Then from April 1934, to clear numbers for the new Stanier 4-6-0's, the Princes had 20,000 added to their numbers, but as withdrawals had begun in September 1933 (with 5652 and 5688) forty one of the class did not have that addition. The class became extinct in May 1949 with 25752's withdrawal.
Only one major alteration was made to this class, and although arranged by Beames in the final months of the LNWR, it was not implemented until after the Grouping. Instead of the normal Joy valve motion between the frames, Walschaerts gear outside the frames was provided to operate the inside cylinders. That new motion required the running plate to be raised for most of its length. Engines 964 and 867 were so rebuilt in March 1923, followed by No.56 in March, and No.2340 in April 1924. An interesting new detail on 964 was a combined socket and lamp iron for those above the buffer beam, but socket only, on top of the smokebox. All were changed to LMS lamp irons throughout in 1925, when 964 (retaining that number and unlined black) was also altered to Belpaire firebox, although it reverted to round-top at its next general repair. None of these four changed from LNW to LMS number before September 1926.
The final engine built to LNWR design was a Prince of Wales class with outside Walschaerts valve gear, ordered by the LMS, and completed by Beardmore in February 1924. Painted red, with emblem on cab side, and numbered 5845 it was fitted with PRINCE OF WALES nameplates (new ones - not those from LNW 819) whilst displayed on the Beardmore stand in the British Empire Exhibition at Wembley, open from 23rd April to 1st November 1924. Later that month, the LMS added it to stock, when the new nameplates were removed, and it was then nameless to withdrawal. To avoid duplication, 819's nameplates were taken off in 1924, but were restored in November 1924 when out from repair, and renumbered 5600. No.5845 was built with Belpaire firebox, on which were pop safety valves, but in 1933-35 carried a boiler with round-top firebox, actually one of the 1911 type with only two washout plugs, although its Ramsbottom valves had been changed to pops. Whilst on exhibition at Wembley, 5845's buffer beam lamp irons were standard LMS type, but curiously, that on smokebox top was an LNW socket, changed later by Crewe to an iron. In January 1935 the number was changed to 25845, and it was not withdrawn until November 1947, the other four with Walschaerts gear having all gone by December 1936.
In March 1948, British Railways allotted their numbers 58000-58003 to LMS 25648, 25673, 25752 and 25787, but none were applied before withdrawal.

(below) **446 PEGASUS was one of the next twenty, built by N.B.Loco.Co from Oct.1915 to Jan.1916, but Crewe built the tenders, and here 446 has changed to the 1910 design. Pyrometer outlet was provided but experience had shown it was not needed. Cooke sandshield was fitted from new and they had full lining. Maker can be identified by their works number on circular plate on the smokebox, but the plate on the cab still had the usual CREWE WORKS on it.**

PRINCE OF WALES CLASS 4-6-0 PASSENGER ENGINES

LNW	NAME	Built	LMS No.	Applied	To 2XXXX	Withdrawn
819	*PRINCE OF WALES*	10/11	5600	10/24	—	10/33
1388	*ANDROMEDA*	10/11	5601	2/27	4/34	3/35
1452	*BONAVENTURE*	10/11	5602	5/26	5/34	6/37
1454	*COQUETTE*	11/11	5603	5/27	4/34	1/35
1537	*ENCHANTRESS*	11/11	5604	11/26	5/34	10/34
1691	*PATHFINDER*	11/11	5605	6/27	5/34	11/34
1704	*CONQUEROR*	11/11	5606	2/27	—	10/33
1721	*DEFIANCE*	11/11	5607	4/26	6/34	12/34
2021	*WOLVERINE*	12/11	5608	4/26	5/34	2/35
2359	*HERMIONE*	12/11	5609	8/27	—	10/33
362	*ROBERT SOUTHEY*	10/13	5610	4/27	—	10/33
892	*CHARLES WOLFE*	10/13	5611	3/27	7/34	6/35
1081	*JOHN KEATS*	10/13	5612	2/26	7/34	1/36
1089	*SYDNEY SMITH*	10/13	5613	11/26	5/34	2/35
1134	*VICTOR HUGO*	10/13	5614	6/26	5/34	12/34
2040	*OLIVER GOLDSMITH*	11/13	5615	2/27	5/34	3/35
2075	*ROBERT BURNS*	11/13	5616	2/27	5/34	11/34
321	*HENRY W.LONGFELLOW*	11/13	5617	3/27	5/34	1/35
479	*THOMAS B.MACAULAY*	12/13	5618	5/27	5/34	2/35
951	*BULWER LYTTON*	12/13	5619	5/27	5/34	8/34
2198	*JOHN RUSKIN*	11/13	5620	4/27	5/34	3/36
2205	*THOMAS MOORE*	11/13	5621	1/27	5/34	8/34
2213	*CHARLES KINGSLEY*	11/13	5622	4/27	—	10/33
1679	*LORD BYRON*	12/13	5623	11/27	5/34	5/35
2249	*THOMAS CAMPBELL*	12/13	5624	3/27	5/34	3/37
2283	*ROBERT L.STEVENSON*	12/13	5625	4/27	5/34	12/36
86	*MARK TWAIN*	1/14	5626	1/27	5/34	5/36
146	*LEWIS CARROLL*	1/14	5627	5/27	5/34	7/36
307	*R.B.SHERIDAN*	12/13	5628	6/26	5/34	11/34
637	*THOMAS GRAY*	12/13	5629	5/27	4/34	12/34
979	*W.M.THACKERAY*	1/14	5630	4/26	5/34	9/34
1400	*FELICIA HEMANS*	1/14	5631	2/27	5/34	6/36
964	*BRET HARTE*	2/14	5632	9/26	—	9/33
985	*SIR W.S.GILBERT*	2/14	5633	10/27	6/34	8/35
1321	*WILLIAM COWPER*	2/14	5634	2/27	5/34	9/34
2152	*CHARLES LAMB*	2/14	5635	9/26	—	3/34
2293	*PERCY BYSSHE SHELLEY*	2/14	5636	1/27	4/34	1/35
2377	*EDWARD GIBBON*	2/14	5637	3/27	5/34	12/36
2443	*CHARLES JAMES LEVER*	3/14	5638	4/26	4/34	4/36
2520	*G.P.NEELE*	3/14	5639	9/26	—	10/33
27	*GENERAL JOFFRE*	10/15	5640	2/27	5/34	2/37
88	*CZAR OF RUSSIA*	10/15	5641	7/26	5/34	9/36
122	*KING OF THE BELGIANS*	11/15	5642	3/27	5/34	3/36
160	*KING OF SERBIA*	11/15	5643	11/26	5/34	10/34
185	*KING OF ITALY*	11/15	5644	12/26	5/34	3/36
877	*RAYMOND POINCARE*	11/15	5645	8/26	5/34	6/36
1333	*SIR JOHN FRENCH*	11/15	5646	10/26	5/34	12/34
2275	*EDITH CAVELL*	11/15	5647	2/27	5/34	1/35
2396	*QUEEN OF THE BELGIANS*	12/15	5648	5/27	5/34	10/48
2408	*ADMIRAL JELLICOE*	12/15	5649	11/27	—	10/33
606	*CASTOR*	1/16	5650	3/24	5/34	4/36
745	*PLUTO*	1/16	5651	5/26	5/34	7/34
810	*ONYX*	1/16	5652	1/27	—	9/33
1352	*THE NILE*	1/16	5653	5/27	5/34	10/35
1379	*WITCH*	1/16	5654	3/27	6/34	3/35
1384	*SMEATON*	1/16	5655	4/26	5/34	12/34
1084	*SHARK*	1/16	5656	3/26	4/34	8/38
1346	*TRENT*	1/16	5657	4/27	4/34	4/36
2417	*ATLAS (removed 8/33)*	1/16	5658	1/27	5/34	10/35
2442	*ODIN*	2/16	5659	3/27	4/34	3/35
90	*KESTREL*	12/15	5660	10/26	5/34	8/36
95	*GALLIPOLI*	3/16	5661	6/26	4/34	2/35
126	*ANZAC*	3/16	5662	3/24	8/34	8/36

LNW	NAME	Built	LMS No.	Applied	To 2XXXX	Withdrawn
136	*MINERVA*	10/15	5663	6/27	5/34	1/35
173	*LIVINGSTONE*	10/15	5664	8/27	6/34	2/35
233	*SUVLA BAY*	3/16	5665	5/27	6/34	4/36
257	*PLYNLIMMON*	11/15	5666	5/26	—	9/34
401	*ZAMIEL*	12/15	5667	5/27	—	11/34
446	*PEGASUS*	11/15	5668	1/24	6/34	8/35
525	*VULCAN*	12/15	5669	7/27	5/34	4/37
610	*ALBION*	12/15	5670	4/27	10/34	10/35
849	*ARETHUSA (removed 9/36)*	3/16	5671	5/26	5/34	12/36
867	*CONDOR (removed 8/33)*	1/16	5672	10/26	4/34	12/36
1100	*LUSITANIA*	3/16	5673	11/27	8/34	1/49
1132	*SCOTT*	1/16	5674	4/26	2/35	2/46
1466	*SPHINX*	1/16	5675	7/26	5/35	8/36
1734	*PETREL*	1/16	5676	5/27	7/34	4/35
1749	*PRECEDENT*	11/15	5677	5/27	—	1/35
2055	*MILTON*	1/16	5678	12/26	5/34	4/35
2063	*HIBERNIA*	11/15	5679	6/27	7/34	5/35
2175	*LOADSTONE*	11/15	5680	5/27	3/35	6/37
2203	*FALSTAFF*	11/15	5681	3/24	10/34	6/35
2329	*SAMSON (removed 8/33)*	1/16	5682	3/27	6/34	4/35
1324	*FALABA*	4/16	5683	5/27	1/35	1/46
2092	*ARABIC*	4/16	5684	6/27	4/35	3/36
2276	*PERSIA*	4/16	5685	2/28	5/34	8/36
2295	*ANGLIA*	4/16	5686	11/23	—	11/34
2300	*HOTSPUR*	12/15	5687	3/27	—	9/34
2340	*TARA*	4/16	5688	3/27	—	9/33
2392	*CALIBAN*	12/15	5689	5/28	8/34	9/36
28	—	1/19	5690	3/28	5/34	11/34
263	—	1/19	5691	3/27	9/34	9/36
295	—	1/19	5692	11/23	1/35	7/37
391	—	1/19	5693	10/26	5/34	5/37

267 PLYNLIMMON was an N.B.Loco. built but here has had two post-war additions - the Beames oilbox on boiler handrail, and the cross-rail on cab side, both put on about 1921. These 20 were similar to those Crewe built except they did not have oilboxes at the front. Tender is the type introduced for this class. Screw coupling at front end is missing.

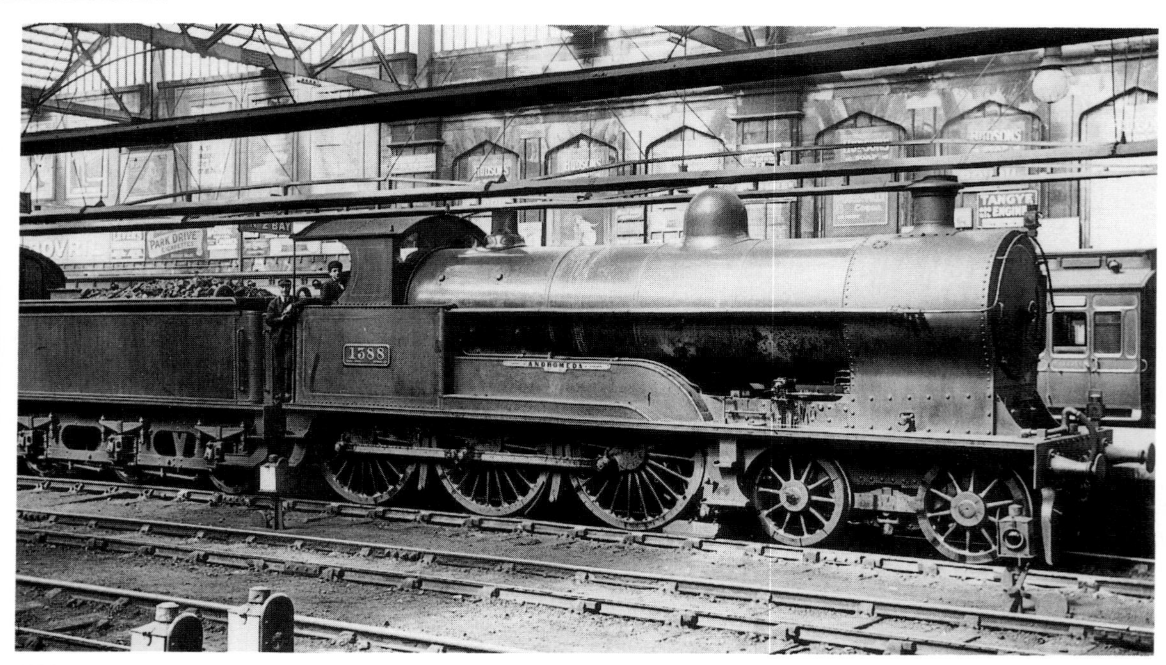

1388 ANDROMEDA was the second one built and here in Carlisle station is still fitted with oil boxes at the front, but has had pyrometer connection removed. Cooke sandshield has been fitted, and tender changed to the design introduced in 1916.

LNW	NAME	Built	LMS No.	Applied	To 2XXXX	Withdrawn
740	—	1/19	5694	8/26	4/34	11/47
805	—	1/19	5695	3/27	7/34	11/34
863	—	1/19	5696	4/26	5/34	12/34
940	*RICHARD COBDEN (named 6/22)*	1/19	5697	6/28	4/34	7/36
1196	—	1/19	5698	6/28	11/34	1/36
1546	—	2/19	5699	5/27	5/34	11/35
621	*TELFORD (named 4/22)*	2/19	5700	5/27	9/34	3/36
707	—	2/19	5701	3/27	6/34	4/35
1373	—	2/19	5702	4/26	11/34	5/36
1453	—	3/19	5703	7/26	6/34	9/34
1584	*SCOTIA (named 5/22)*	3/19	5704	11/27	9/34	9/36
57	—	3/19	5705	11/26	10/34	3/35
504	*CANNING (named 8/22)*	3/19	5706	1/27	5/35	12/36
974	*HAMPDEN (named 2/22)*	3/19	5707	9/27	6/34	4/35
1673	—	3/19	5708	2/27	4/34	8/36
2184	—	3/19	5709	9/26	—	12/34
33	—	4/19	5710	9/26	7/34	4/35
388	—	4/19	5711	11/27	1/35	4/35
1123	—	4/19	5712	4/26	10/34	4/37
1215	—	4/19	5713	1/27	—	6/35
1351	—	4/19	5714	9/27	—	5/35
1437	—	5/19	5715	3/27	—	2/35
1670	—	5/19	5716	5/27	1/35	8/35
1732	—	5/19	5717	1/28	6/34	6/36
2073	—	5/19	5718	6/27	4/35	6/36
2285	—	5/19	5719	11/26	—	11/34
444	—	5/19	5720	4/27	6/34	11/35
497	—	6/19	5721	4/27	12/34	7/36
501	—	6/19	5722	3/27	5/35	3/48
522	*STENTOR (named 7/22)*	6/19	5723	4/27	6/34	1/36
601	—	6/19	5724	5/27	5/34	6/35
783	—	6/19	5725	12/26	4/34	12/45
56	—	6/19	5726	2/27	4/35	7/36
924	—	6/19	5727	2/27	4/34	5/35
1125	—	7/19	5728	6/24	8/34	1/36
1290	*LUCKNOW (named 7/22)*	7/19	5729	2/24	8/34	2/35
1307	—	7/19	5730	10/26	3/34	12/36

LNW	NAME	Built	LMS No.	Applied	To 2XXXX	Withdrawn
67	—	7/19	5731	4/26	6/34	8/35
635	—	8/19	5732	3/27	8/34	11/38
686	—	8/19	5733	3/27	11/34	8/35
812	—	8/19	5734	11/26	1/35	7/35
969	—	8/19	5735	5/27	—	9/34
1325	*DISRAELI (named 5/22)*	8/19	5736	3/27	5/34	6/35
1341	—	8/19	5737	1/27	9/34	2/36
1355	—	9/19	5738	11/23	4/34	5/35
1620	—	9/19	5739	12/27	12/34	3/36
35	—	9/19	5740	1/28	11/34	12/35
395	—	9/19	5741	6/26	11/34	1/36
487	—	9/19	5742	3/27	—	3/35
1178	*PRINCE ALBERT (named 2/22)*	9/19	5743	2/26	—	9/34
889	—	10/19	5744	4/27	5/34	3/36
1113	—	10/19	5745	2/26	—	12/34
1408	—	10/19	5746	4/26	10/34	2/36
1422	—	10/19	5747	11/23	10/34	4/36
1478	—	10/19	5748	2/28	3/34	10/36
1535	—	10/19	5749	12/26	11/34	1/46
1542	*MARATHON (named 8/22)*	11/19	5750	6/26	10/34	3/36
1549	—	11/19	5751	8/25	1/35	7/44
1557	—	11/19	5752	5/27	6/34	5/49
1694	*PREMIER (named 8/22)*	11/19	5753	12/27	5/34	2/36
2516	*DALTON (named 8/22)*	11/19	5754	1/28	6/34	5/35
120	*	6/21	5755	3/27	—	11/34
123	*	8/21	5756	3/27	4/34	12/38
125	*	8/21	5757	12/26	11/34	9/36
129	*	8/21	5758	3/27	8/34	11/34
135	*	8/21	5759	5/27	5/34	6/35
140	*	8/21	5760	4/27	—	10/34
141	*	8/21	5761	5/27	—	12/34
142	*	8/21	5762	2/27	5/35	4/36
145	*	8/21	5763	8/27	12/34	9/39
148	*	8/21	5764	10/27	5/34	6/36
224	*	8/21	5765	4/27	—	12/34
227	*	8/21	5766	7/27	11/34	8/35
232	*	9/21	5767	3/27	5/34	6/37
237	*	9/21	5768	11/26	4/34	4/37
239	*	9/21	5769	4/27	4/34	1/36
240	*	9/21	5770	3/24	—	4/35
241	*	9/21	5771	12/27	7/34	3/36
242	*	9/21	5772	2/27	10/34	3/36
243	*	9/21	5773	9/26	5/35	5/37
244	*	9/21	5774	4/26	—	10/34
246	*	9/21	5775	2/27	4/34	11/47
247	*	9/21	5776	2/24	4/34	2/36
248	*	9/21	5777	9/23	3/35	3/37
249	*	10/21	5778	5/27	—	9/34
251	*	10/21	5779	11/26	5/34	6/37
252	*	10/21	5780	5/27	9/34	6/37
258	*	10/21	5781	11/26	6/34	3/36
259	*	10/21	5782	3/27	—	12/34
261	*	10/21	5783	8/26	—	12/34
266	*	10/21	5784	12/26	8/34	8/36
267	*	10/21	5785	6/24	5/34	5/36
268	*	10/21	5786	5/27	—	12/34
269	*	10/21	5787	12/26	8/34	5/48
270	*	11/21	5788	2/24	4/34	4/37
272	*	11/21	5789	9/27	—	3/34
273	*	11/21	5790	3/27	4/35	10/36
274	*	11/21	5791	9/23	10/35	12/47
394	*	10/21	5792	5/27	6/34	5/37
277	*	11/21	5793	1/27	1/35	5/35
281	*	11/21	5794	8/27	5/35	12/36

LNW	NAME	Built	LMS No.	Applied	To 2XXXX	Withdrawn
284	*	11/21	5795	9/23	10/34	1/36
292	*	11/21	5796	2/27	5/34	7/36
293	*	11/21	5797	4/26	5/34	6/47
296	*	11/21	5798	2/27	6/34	6/45
313	*	11/21	5799	4/27	1/35	7/35
324	*	11/21	5800	8/28	4/34	4/37
325	*	12/21	5801	1/27	11/34	3/36
331	*	12/21	5802	4/27	2/35	3/47
355	*	12/21	5803	2/28	6/35	3/36
357	*	12/21	5804	5/27	5/34	2/46
359	*	12/21	5805	3/27	5/34	6/45
435	*	12/21	5806	10/27	—	10/34
436	*	12/21	5807	11/23	—	11/34
438	*	12/21	5808	3/27	5/34	4/35
440	*	12/21	5809	9/23	—	11/34
442	*	12/21	5810	3/27	4/34	5/35
443	*	12/21	5811	5/27	6/34	1/35
452	*	12/21	5812	5/27	2/35	12/36
483	*	12/21	5813	5/24	6/34	5/36
489	*	12/21	5814	3/24	—	2/35
490	*	12/21	5815	11/23	3/34	7/35
492	*	2/22	5816	5/27	1/35	3/36
17	*	2/22	5817	8/27	4/34	3/36
153	*	2/22	5818	11/27	8/34	8/46
198	*	2/22	5819	8/26	11/34	2/37
354	*	2/22	5820	9/28	6/34	4/36
491	*	1/22	5821	12/26	6/34	3/37
493	*	1/22	5822	5/27	6/34	3/36
518	*	2/22	5823	2/28	4/34	3/36
551	*	2/22	5824	8/26	—	11/34
554	*	2/22	5825	3/27	6/35	12/36
549	*	2/22	5826	9/23	7/34	2/36
557	*	1/22	5827	9/26	4/34	3/48
558	*	2/22	5828	4/27	4/35	11/36
778	*	3/22	5829	6/24	4/34	1/37
1099	*	3/22	5830	11/27	8/34	8/36
1179	*	3/22	5831	9/26	7/34	5/35
1316	*	3/22	5832	4/27	11/34	10/36
1339	*	3/22	5833	4/27	4/34	6/37
53	*	3/22	5834	9/23	8/34	10/36
197	*	3/22	5835	2/27	8/34	1/36
433	*	4/22	5836	1/27	6/34	3/36
614	*	4/22	5837	2/28	8/34	3/35
1083	*	4/22	5838	2/24	10/34	5/35
1320	*	4/22	5839	6/24	11/34	1/37
1349	*	3/22	5840	9/27	7/34	1/36
1323	*	4/22	5841	4/26	3/34	9/47
1344	*	4/22	5842	12/26	8/34	6/36
1742	*	4/22	5843	9/23	3/34	8/36
2043	*	4/22	5844	3/27	5/34	9/36

* *All these were built by Beardmore at Dalmuir and none were given a name.*

In March 1948, BR allotted numbers 58000-58003 to LMS 25648, 25673, 25752 and 25787, but none were applied before withdrawal.

5845 was also added to this class by the LMS. Built in February 1924 for the Wembley Exhibition, it was taken into stock in November 1924. Renumbered 25845 in September 1934, it was withdrawn in November 1947.

863 shows the right hand side of the 1919 Crewe batch, on which the lubrication of the motion had a change; note the pipe to the front of the smokebox on both sides.

889 built at Crewe in October 1919, but seen here in 1923, has been changed to Belpaire firebox with pop safety valves; has acquired Beames oilbox and cab rail, but snifter is blanked off. Engine has lining, but not tender, and curiously, an LMS date plate has been put on splasher the LNW armorial being obliterated. Note mechanical lubricator has no hand control. *Real Photos.*

1083 was built by Beardmore in Glasgow during April 1922, and their rectangular works plate was fitted on smokebox below the vacuum pipe entry but has been taken off. Cab rail is fitted but not Beames oilbox, and the top lamp iron is clear to see.

1704 CONQUEROR, the sixth built, has had oil boxes at front removed, Beames oilbox, and cab rail added, also tender changed to 1910 type, but in 1923 got Belpaire firebox with four plugs and Ross pop safety valves. Note oil feed pipes now go into steam chest at side instead of at the back.

27 GENERAL JOFFRE was the first of the thirty built at Crewe in 1915/16, but in 1923 had boiler changed to Belpaire with pop safety valves, and by then, Beames oilbox, and cab rail had been added, also tender changed to 1916 design. Note it still has snifter, and pyrometer outlet cover, and is plain black. These thirty were the last to be built with sandbox below the running plate. Cab roof has been altered to Midland gauge and it is at Derby.

487 was one of the sixty five Crewe built from January to November 1919, none of which were named before 1922, and all were turned out in plain black but had armorial. Their leading sandbox was placed above the running plate adjacent to the splasher, and they were fitted with a vertical drain pipe to the snifter.

1351 built at Crewe in April 1919 only had plain black painting, but when repaired in 1921, had Beames oilbox put on, and it was lined out fully. Note that it still lacked handrail across cab.

One of the engines built 1921/22 by Wm. Beardmore in Glasgow, being delivered by the Caledonian's '908' class No.916. The 'Caley' loading gauge maximum height was 12' 11" against the LNW 13' 6" which explains the denuded appearance of the LNW engine.

5615 OLIVER GOLDSMITH has the Belpaire firebox boiler with four washout plugs on each side which Beames introduced in 1923. LNW shed plate 15 (Crewe) has been moved from the cab roof to the smokebox door.

5683 FALABA (NOT TO BE MOVED) is coupled with a 1912 design tender introduced for G1 and this class, which had a flared coping with double beading instead of coal rails. They were vacuum braked with blocks at the rear of the tender wheels.

5621 THOMAS MOORE has boiler with two plugs, but Ross pops (on the same seating) have replaced the Ramsbottom safety valves. Its shed was 15 which was that of Crewe. Note change to R.O.D. tender. *A.G.Ellis.*

5668 PEGASUS another of the class attached to R.O.D. tender which carried a ton of coal and 800 gallons of water more than the largest LNW tender.

25841 at Crewe North shed in August 1938 still had Cooke taper shank, solid spindle buffers on its damaged front end, but as it remained in use until September 1947, its replacement type would probably be Stanier.

5777 here at Blackpool North shed in September 1933 has arrived on an excursion for the Illuminations, and has had its Cooke buffers replaced by a Stanier design which differed by having square flange, parallel shank, and hollow spindle, giving the appearance of being stronger.

25604 ENCHANTRESS at Liverpool Edge Hill in July 1934 shows tender as well as engine normally had Cooke taper shank buffers. Its '2' is clearly a shed addition. *W.L.Good.*

25624 THOMAS CAMPBELL at Rugby on 1st December 1935 has also been changed to Stanier buffers, used when needed on this class. *W.L.Good.*

5756 in Crewe works on 16th July 1933 has the customary style of smokebox door with wheel and handle fastening. Air leakage was avoided by extra help from dog clips, usually four, but 5756 has an extra one at the bottom. The LNW shed plate is 27 for Preston. *W.L.Good.*

5659 ODIN at Rugby station on 2nd April 1932, was one of six noted with this type door fastened only by eight dog clips, and with lamp iron moved on to the door. The others were 25608 WOLVERINE in February 1935, 25788 in August 1936, also 5640 (16.7.33), 25681 (14.4.35) and 25691 (14.9.35).

25695 at Crewe works on 22nd July 1934 has had its LNW 16 (Longsight) shed plate moved from their position at rear edge of cab roof on to smokebox door, the earliest one so noted being on 28th June 1931. 2" high black figures were on a 5" x $3^{1}/_{2}$" white enamelled oval plate. *W.L.Good.*

5651 PLUTO at Shrewsbury shed (LNW 30 plate) on 20th August 1933 is as built to the LNW load gauge, which allowed a 9' 0" width up to 11' 0" at the sides, which was 3" higher than on the Midland. *W.L.Good.*

25627 LEWIS CARROLL at Chester 20th August 1934 shows how the cab roof corners had to be altered to pass Midland gauge. At least sixty five were so changed, four as early as 1923, but the majority from 1928 to 1933.

2392 CALIBAN, at Longsight shed, is fitted with two cylindrical tanks for oil fuel in May 1926, and has escaped loss of its LNW number plate; it was not renumbered to 5689 until May 1928. Thirty six of the class are recorded as having been fitted to burn oil fuel during the long coal strike of 1926.

5607 DEFIANCE was adapted to burn oil fuel during the coal strike of 1926, for which its tender carried these two cylindrical tanks. In April 1926 its LNW number plate was taken off, and the new number was painted on the space vacated, hence their small size, only six inches, the same size as the figures cast on the brass plates. *A.G.Ellis.*

2275 EDITH CAVELL, here calling at Stalybridge on a Leeds-Liverpool express, has the standard LNW lamp sockets which, apart from the ninety built by Beardmore, were in general use until the mid-1920's.

444 built by Crewe in May 1919 changed to this Belpaire firebox in April 1925, but not to LMS 5720 until April 1927. The necessary cab alteration included modification to pass MR gauge, also a curved instead of straight rain strip. Engine is plain black but the tender has LNW lining.

5671 ARETHUSA also had its 849 LNW plate removed, in May 1926, but due to a different type of tender, its rectangular tank was shorter. Its cab is devoid of any numbering but a plate has been fitted on the smokebox door.

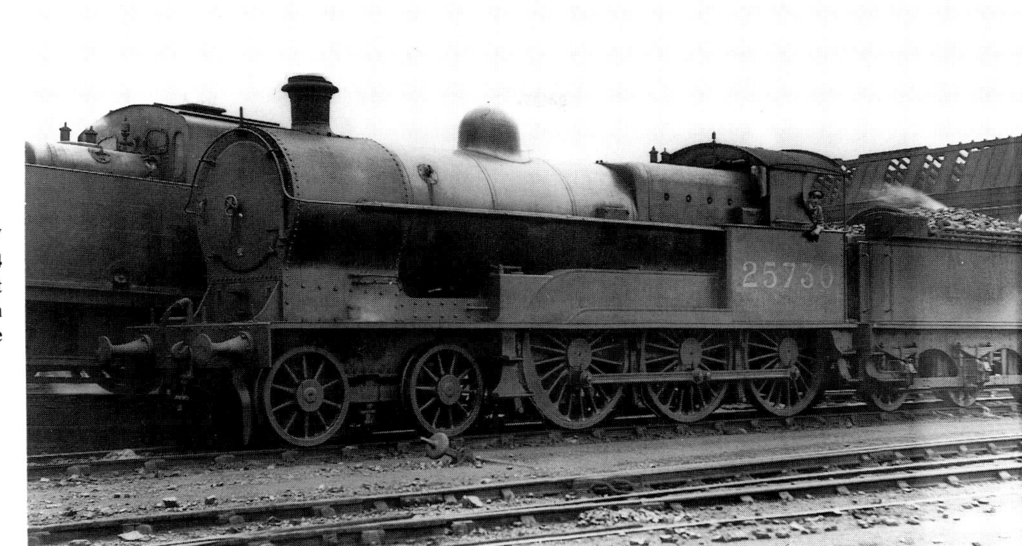

25730 at Patricroft shed (LNW shed plate 34) on 24th June 1934 has been fitted on the first cleading band with an outlet from the boiler for which its purpose has not yet been identified.

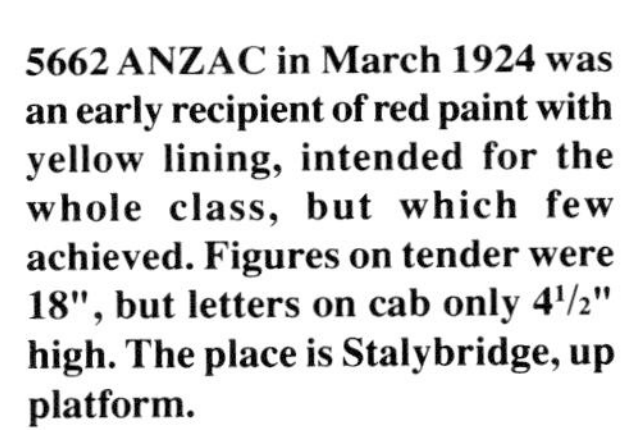
5662 ANZAC in March 1924 was an early recipient of red paint with yellow lining, intended for the whole class, but which few achieved. Figures on tender were 18", but letters on cab only 4½" high. The place is Stalybridge, up platform.

5807 engine (identified from smokebox plate) took that number in November 1923 from LNW 436, but later got tender 5662. The LNW custom of changing tender without restriction inevitably caused confusion after the LMS decided to put the number on the tender in Midland style.

5788 got that number and red painting in February 1924, and was the subject of a trial to give changeability to the tender numbering. Rails put on the tender allowed individual figures to be slotted in. The experiment quickly proved either impractical or undesirable, or both, because it was not extended to others, but tenders still had 18" figures painted on until well into 1927.

5839, at Derby, so renumbered and painted red in June 1924, got the LMS 14" diameter armorial on the cab instead of letters, and that was standard style until late 1927 where repainting was possible.

5607 DEFIANCE in late 1926 when it ceased to be oil fired, remained black, and without lining, but the black tender kept LNW lining, despite the 18" figures then painted on it. Note cab has been altered to pass Midland gauge.

5843 here at Liverpool's exL&Y Bank Hall engine shed, on 16th August 1924, must have had regular attention from cleaners to be so spruce almost a year after it was painted in this red livery.

5809 (like 5843) was amongst the first of this class to change from LNW black to LMS red painting, and also the latter's numbering, which it acquired in September 1923.

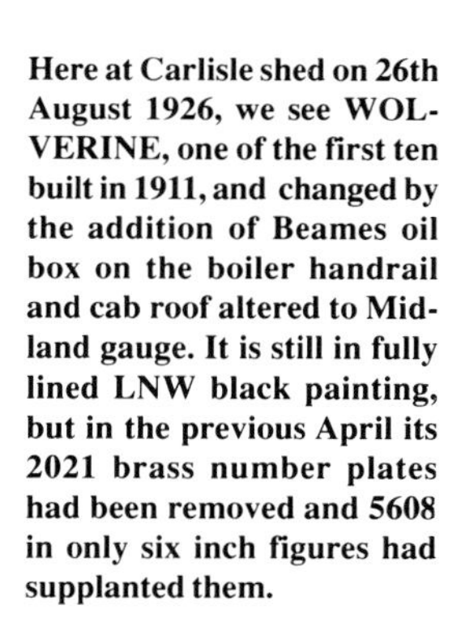

Here at Carlisle shed on 26th August 1926, we see WOLVERINE, one of the first ten built in 1911, and changed by the addition of Beames oil box on the boiler handrail and cab roof altered to Midland gauge. It is still in fully lined LNW black painting, but in the previous April its 2021 brass number plates had been removed and 5608 in only six inch figures had supplanted them.

With almost 250 engines in the class, some mixed traffic duties inevitably came their way, as shown here by 5661 GALLIPOLI on this down goods near Stafford whilst 5661 was fitted for oil firing. That was installed in June 1926, when its LNW 95 number plates were taken off and 5661 in six inch figures replaced them.

5616 ROBERT BURNS on this down 11-coach express is picking up water from the troughs at Whitmore on 7th June 1930. By then the livery style had settled at the cab figures matching the fourteen inch high lettering on the tender. *W.L.Good.*

The work of the class was widely spread, and 5730 here in the 1930's is about to depart from Holyhead with an express passenger train.

Somewhat of a problem picture is presented by 5779 at Carnforth (Midland) shed on 8th August 1930. Its shed allocation plate is still mounted at the rear of the cab roof so provides no clue, but its cab roof edges have *not* been altered to suit Midland load gauge.

25674 SCOTT has just completed its repair at Crewe in 1938, and its 5C shed plate shows that it was allocated to Stafford. It was one of the first to be altered to Midland load gauge, in August 1923, but here it is changed to Belpaire firebox and Stanier buffers. *W.L.Good.*

25602 BONAVENTURE is at Aston shed on 2nd May 1937, only a month before withdrawal. It is painted unlined black and although it had 2XXXX addition from May 1934, the cab panel appears to have been singled out for recent painting to carry the Midland style figures with back shading to them.

25725, of shed 29, is at Crewe South on 28th April 1934 after completing a repair at Crewe Works. In unlined black, it has Midland style numerals which have no back shading. In line with current custom the LNW shed plate has been moved to the smokebox door. At this latest repair 25725 had changed to Stanier buffers, an early application of that type.

5624 THOMAS CAMPBELL got that number in March 1927 by 10" figures on the cab, and had a cast plate put on the smokebox door. Both engine and tender were in black without lining, but here the tender has the standard 14" LMS on it. *A.G.Ellis.*

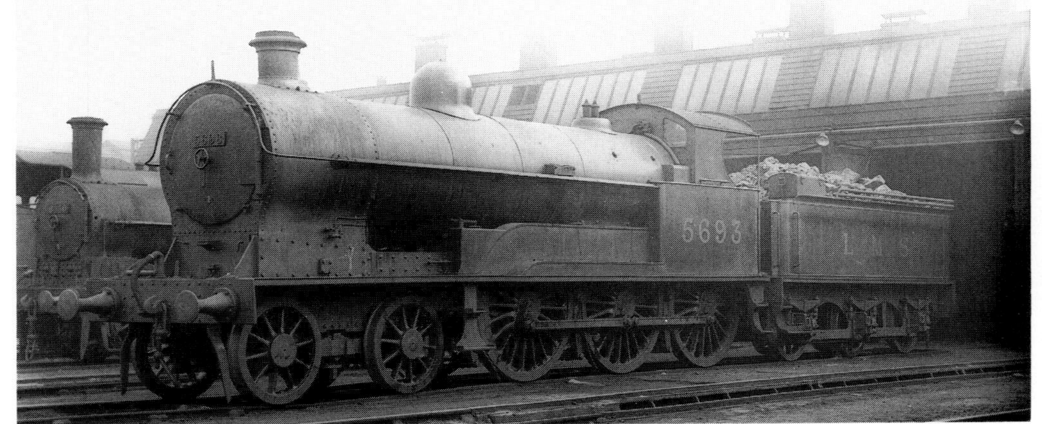

5693 changed to that number in October 1926 when smokebox plates were still being fitted by Crewe Works; here 15th April 1934 at Crewe South shed it has matching 14" characters, standard from the end of 1927, but somewhat unusually, retains smokebox plate. *W.L.Good.*

No.25625 ROBERT L. STEVENSON was reboilered in 1935 to Belpaire firebox, when Crewe then centred the number on the cab (since April 1934 it had worn the shed-applied 2) and applied shaded figures and letters as seen at Rugby on 14th September 1935.

5619 BULWER LYTTON at Crewe North shed on 15th April 1934 has had drain pipe fitted to vacuum ejector exhaust pipe. The drain pipe extends down the side of the bogie.

5667 ZAMIEL has the altered lubricator arrangement but does not have vacuum ejector exhaust drain pipe. The smokebox number plate has been removed but its fixing bolts are still to be seen.

5687 HOTSPUR at Crewe North shed in July 1933 shows the altered steam chest lubrication arrangement, with vertical pipe. *Photomatic.*

25631 FELICIA HEMANS at Crewe had leading coupled wheel balance weight with the more usual crescent shape spanning six spokes. *Photomatic.*

25763 at Llandudno Junction in August 1935 clearly shows the relative positions of the balance weights in all three pairs of coupled wheels.

25612 JOHN KEATS on an express at Northampton (Castle) 5th May 1935 has been fitted with pyrometer connection from smokebox outlet to cab. It was unusual to see one fitted twenty years after they were found to be un-necessary, when experience of superheating was gained.

25827 here at Crewe North shed on 19th September 1937 was also fitted with pyrometer connection from smokebox to cab, and it is unlikely to be the same boiler, because of the different firebox type.

86 MARK TWAIN with a special goods on the Caledonian to the north of Carlisle. Note that it still has oil boxes at front of steam chest, and is unchanged from new in all details. It carries no lamp to indicate class of train, the board in the top lamp bracket apparently serving that purpose. Note spare lamp stowed on side of smokebox.

2249 THOMAS CAMPBELL heads a down express on the water troughs at Dillicar. This is what and where they were designed to work and typical of the LNWR as I first knew it.

259 PLYNLIMMON, on an express to Euston, approaching Kenton in early LMS days, only one coach still having LNW colours.

525 VULCAN is leaving Lancaster for Euston on *THE LAKES EXPRESS* from Keswick and from Windermere in 1924.

5712 on 15th September 1930 has the 3.30 p.m. from Manchester to Liverpool special in connection with the Centenary of the opening of that line. No lamps are carried but there is a shield in each of the four positions indicating a Royal train. The right hand one shows Prince of Wales feathers and his ermine-trimmed hat appears on the top shield. A bowler hat in the cab also is of significance, but no Royalty graced the occasion.
LCGB Ken Nunn Collection.

25644 KING OF ITALY is leaving Oxenholme with the Keswick portion of *THE LAKES EXPRESS* in the 1935 summer.

25737 leaves Cambridge with a stopping train for Bletchley and a carries 2B (Nuneaton) shedplate; also a 1935 picture.

25751 as renumbered in January 1935, and with 4A (Bletchley) shed plate has four Great Western coaches on an Oxford train.

(above) **5827 of Stafford shed with number on cab from March 1928 has engine in red painting but tender seems to be black. This is a problem picture, because although stationary, the train is working "wrong line", unless the up and down lines are paired slow and fast.**

25722 at Berkhamsted on Friday 26th July 1940 has called there with a local train from Euston to Bletchley. Note the sans-serif 10" numerals and 14" letters which were used from April 1936 but discarded a year later.
H.C.Casserley.

25822 so numbered in June 1934, and in that summer, is taking water from the track troughs at Brock, 8 miles north of Preston, where its 27 plate showed it to be shedded. The varied roof line of the coaches on this down express was very typical of even main line expresses.

964 BRET HARTE shows the original condition of this engine which, in November 1922 was selected as the first to be altered for trial of outside Walschaerts valve gear to operate its existing inside cylinders.

964 BRET HARTE as it returned to traffic in March 1923 retaining original type boiler but with tender changed from 1911 to 1916 design. The altered valve gear needed a raised running plate. Note combined socket and iron for the buffer beam lampholders.

964 whilst still with that LNW number (it changed to LMS 5632 in September 1926) had boiler changed to one with Belpaire firebox, and its cab roof was modified to permit it to pass MR load gauge. *Real Photos.*

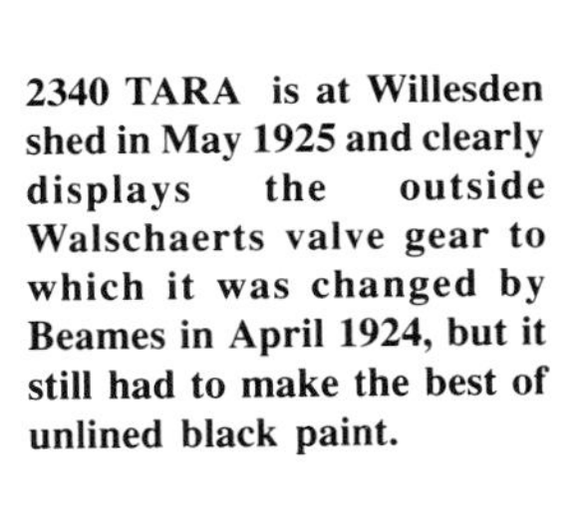

2340 TARA is at Willesden shed in May 1925 and clearly displays the outside Walschaerts valve gear to which it was changed by Beames in April 1924, but it still had to make the best of unlined black paint.

2340 TARA had its boiler changed to one with pops and four plugs, and here with indicator shelter is being evaluated. Whatever the result, no more were so changed. In March 1927 the engine reverted to its original design boiler but with pop safety valves not Ramsbottom. At the same time it got its LMS number 5688. *R.S.Carpenter.*

5845 although of entirely LNW design was not built until February 1924, and then by Wm.Beardmore in Glasgow to appear on their stand in the British Empire Exhibition at Wembley. The LMS did not put it into stock until November 1924, but must have agreed to buy it, when it was named, numbered and painted to suit. A normal rectangular Beardmore works number plate (showing 304) is on the side of the smokebox.

5726 is approaching Huddersfield station on an express from Leeds to Manchester (Exchange), almost surely the return working for a Shrewsbury shedded engine which had arrived in Leeds on the 2.40 a.m. mail train from Swansea.

964 BRET HARTE at Edge Hill is assisting Claughton 650 LORD RATHMORE on this Liverpool-London express, but probably only a convenient way to work it back to Crewe, which was then its home shed.

964 BRET HARTE here is running into Crewe working the up *IRISH MAIL* soon after its March 1923 rebuilding. Note all coaches are still in LNWR painting. *Real Photos.*

5726, never named, was LNW 56 when it became the last to be changed in April 1924, and only became 5726 in February 1927. Here on 20th August 1932 it is at Shrewsbury shed and has their 30 plate. It has original type 2-plug boiler but with pops. Snifting valve at base of smokebox has been blanked off, and tender is the 1905 type with two open coal rails. *W.L.Good.*

5845 from new had lamp irons, not sockets, and its cab roof enabled it to pass MR gauge, and had curved rain strip. Two purely Beames features were Belpaire firebox, and oil boxes on the handrails on both sides. Before putting it in traffic the LMS removed the nameplates, which were then discarded.

5845 at some time in the early 1930's had a boiler change to one with round-top firebox which had only two washout plugs, but had been changed to pop safety valves, on a Ramsbottom mounting. That boiler was carried until 1937 when it reverted to one with Belpaire firebox. 25845 was altered to that number in September 1934, and here at Bletchley 25th June 1938 has had buffers changed to Stanier type. Its 2B plate shows it allocated to Bletchley, having transferred to that shed from Shrewsbury in December 1936.
L.Hanson.

CLAUGHTON 4-CYLINDER 4-6-0 EXPRESS PASSENGER ENGINES

The first engine, No.2222 appeared in January 1913, and included some details which were not perpetuated on those that followed. Its safety valves were the usual pair of Ramsbottom type, but when the next engine came out in May, it had two pairs side by side, with the casing widened to suit, and that became standard on the class. By June 1913, 2222 had been brought into line, another pair being added to it. The tender built with, and for 2222, was the only one to have a double beaded coal guard, the other nine in the first batch only having a one-piece coal guard, which was the style adopted for all subsequent tenders built by the LNWR. No.2222 was also unique in having four windows in the front plate of the cab. It was quickly found that the two small ones above the firebox served no useful purpose, and they were done away with in 1915. In front of the cab, on the left-hand side, 2222 had the brake valve and train pipe connection; the second, and all the later engines had those inside the cab.

On the first ten, in service by July 1913, the lower corners of the front buffer beam were square, but after fouling a platform at Bletchley later that year, they were chamfered, a little at first, but then increased, and all were so treated. Whilst running its trials in January 1913, No.2222 had the customary socket holders for the lamps, but in February, whilst in works for painting and lining, the sockets were replaced by irons. The other nine of the first batch had sockets when new, but from 1915 had combined sockets and irons, but all later engines just had irons. Why Claughtons should differ, when the other LNW engines used sockets until after the Grouping in 1923, has not been discovered.

Most of the first thirty engines (those built to September 1916) were fitted with damper for the superheater, its operating gear being combined with the boiler handrail, and they also had a pyrometer for measuring superheat temperature, the pipe to the gauge in the cab emerging from the right-hand side of the smokebox. It was soon found that neither was really required, and from about 1919, were removed, the later built engines never being so equipped.

In mid-1913 Cooke began to fit the sandshields that he had patented, the purpose of which was to prevent sand being blown from the point of application by side winds. On the first ten, they were fitted only for the leading coupled wheels, but by 1915, they were also being fitted to the sandpipes for the middle coupled wheels. They were still to be seen at the end of the LNWR, but were already being discarded, and in July 1923, the first Claughton to be painted in LMS livery did not have them.

Following trials on Precursor 2585, in 1921 Claughton 2222 was fitted to burn oil fuel, but neither its tender nor its oil tank were those which 2585 had used. During the 1921 coal strike, only this one Claughton was changed to oil, but the much longer dispute in 1926 led to thirty seven of the class being equipped for oil instead of coal firing. Beginning with those built in 1920, a short horizontal hand rail was fitted on the cab side; that proved such a boon that these hand rails were quickly added to the sixty of the class built previously.

After Beames succeeded Cooke as C.M.E. in 1920, he decided to

2222 painted shop grey, and running on trial in January 1913 at Manchester London Road. Note that it has only one pair of Ramsbottom safety valves, no cover to reversing gear, no nameplate, no sandshields, no handrail across cab side, and its tender has flared top with double beading, and D shape frame slots. Damper operating gear for superheater it fitted, and on the other side was a pyrometer connection from smokebox to cab. The buffer beam has square lower corners, sockets are fitted for the lamps, the cab front has two small extra windows and brake pipe is outside cab. All these items subsequently changed.

2222 running indicator trials in February 1913, has had lamp irons fitted and sockets removed, and whilst in works grey paint still, nameplate is now fitted.

add more oiling to the coupled wheel bearings, and initially on the Claughtons, small oil boxes each with three feed pipes from them were added behind the boiler hand rails to service the leading and middle coupled axles. They proved useful, but needed augmenting, so larger boxes, again on each side, mounted on the boiler hand rails became standard.

By the time that Stanier buffers were introduced in 1933, unrebuilt Claughtons were being withdrawn rapidly, but at least six 5909, 5912, 5920, 5947, 5951 and 5994 which survived into 1935, were changed to that type, which had parallel shank and square base. Otherwise their original Cooke type with taper shank and circular base was standard fitting.

For smokebox door, all began with wheel and handle, augumented by four dog clips to prevent leakage of air. On the final ten built May/June 1921, Beames added a fifth dog clip at the base of the door. In the early 1930's a slightly larger diameter door began to be used; that had no central fastening, but relied entirely on eight dog clips. It was fitted to at least 5900 and 5990, on which the former kept its smokebox number plate to withdrawal, but the latter only carried one from July 1927 into 1929. These doors also had the upper lamp iron fitted on them, giving easier access than on top of the smokebox. Beginning in 1931, the LNW enamelled shed allocation plate was moved from the rear of cab roof on to the smokebox door, and on some of the engines which had been transferred to Midland Division sheds, their cast type was used instead. The 1935, LMS revised "all-line" shed indication, using a number for the district shed, and a letter suffix for sheds responsible to it saw cast plates with number above and letter below put on smokebox doors but only a handful of unrebuilt Claughtons survived to have that type applied. 5947 and 5951 did so, although both were withdrawn later that year.

The first ten, built in 1913, naturally had full London & North Western Railway lining, as did the first two, Nos.250 and 260 of those built in August 1914. Due to the outbreak of war, No.1131, the third of that batch, entered traffic in unlined black, relieved only by the front buffer beam, and the background to the numberplates being painted red. All the other 118 of the class, built through to June 1921, first had this sombre guise, but full lining was able to be resumed on those repaired and repainted from October 1921. There was one minor exception - the engine chosen to be the LNWR war memorial, and specially numbered 1914, which had been given the normal vermilion background to its number plates, for the official photograph, taken on 22nd May 1920. That was thought to be too bright, and was changed to black before the engine was released to traffic.

Fully lined engines in LNWR livery continued to come out of Crewe until 21st July 1923, when No.5971 (ex 2511) was the first to have LMS red painting, 18" numerals on its tender, and $4^1/_2$" LMS on the cab sides. 5944 done similarly was ex works in September, followed by 5939, 5947 and 5979 in March 1924. Normally there would have been a change from the cab lettering to the circular transfer-applied armorial, but due to the complete re-organisation, and a reluctance to change from black, Crewe Works applied little paint from 1924 to 1926. They did manage to put 5900 SIR GILBERT CLAUGHTON into red, and with armorial, for its participation in the July 1925 Stockton & Darlington Centenary procession, but then descended to the ridiculous. Seven Claughton class (5931, 5949, 5984, 5986, 6001, 6019 and 6028, whilst remaining in black, in April 1926, had their LNW brass number plates removed, and those LMS numbers, only 6" high were hand painted in their place, simply because Crewe had been instructed to speed up their alterations to LMS numbering. Even so, it was not until June 1928 that LNW 183 changed to LMS 6020, to complete the renumbering of the Claughton class.

By June 1926 some red painting was resumed, and by the end of 1927, nearly thirty of the class had been changed to it, with circular armorial on the cab sides. During 1927, at least two, 5932 in February, and 5945 in June, whilst still in unlined black, had their LNW number plates taken off, and those LMS numbers put on the cab in 10". From January 1928 it was made standard for the engine number to be on the cab instead of on the tender, which then carried the Company initials LMS, all in 14" characters. By the time of the first withdrawal, all are believed to have acquired red livery, and that remained standard for this class, both as built, and as fitted with larger boiler, through to the end, even on 6004, which survived until April 1949.

Despite being the most prestigious of the LNWR locomotives, they were not immune from Crewe's policy of regarding any suitable tender as on a common user basis, although no Claughton seems to have been paired with the 1905 design with two open coal rails. The 130 engines even started work with three different tender types. 2222 with a double beaded coal guard, but all the others with only a single. The frames of the twenty built in 1913/4 had tapered rear end and semi-elliptical slots. On those built from July 1916 the rear end was longer with a square vertical edge, and the slots were "square-oval". There were frequent changes of tender type, and from 1927, tenders bought from the R.O.D. (and of G.C.R. design) were put with many Claughtons, particularly with those transferred to work on Midland Division lines because of their greater water and coal capacity.

DEVELOPMENTS INITIATED BY THE L.M.S.

The last Chief Mechanical Engineer of the LNWR, Beames remained in charge at Crewe, and in the early 1920's had made a study of Caprotti poppet valve gear introduced from Italy. In August 1926 he was able to apply it on one of the first batch of Claughtons, which concurrently changed its number from LNW 1327 to LMS 5908. Road testing, and indicator diagrams showed a 20% saving in coal consumption but only that one retaining the original type boiler was so fitted. At less cost, it was found that similar savings could be achieved by changing from one broad to six narrow piston rings on others of the class, so they were made the standard.
Starting in April 1928, twenty Claughtons were fitted with a 6" larger diameter boiler, and on ten of them the Walschaerts valve gear was retained, but nine other engines were changed to Caprotti valve gear, all nineteen being rebuilt during 1928, followed in December by the already Caprotti fitted 5908 getting larger boiler.
That bigger boiler caused problems at first by smoke and steam drifting along it, impairing forward visibility for the driver, and smoke deflectors had to be put on. Straight sided ones were first tried, but better results were obtained if the top portion was sloped inward, so that was adopted as standard.
In early 1932 No.5912 and 6001 were fitted with Kylala blastpipe, and also a larger diameter chimney in consequence, but only those two were so fitted and they were withdrawn in February 1935 and October 1934 respectively.
The acquisition by the LMS of fifty "Royal Scot" class locomotives in 1927 made the Claughtons redundant for working West Coast main line expresses, so in 1928 about twenty five were transferred to the Midland Division to work between St Pancras, Leeds, and Carlisle. That line's loading gauge only permitted 10' 9" vertical height to the start of the curved part, whereas on the LNW it was 11' 0", so for use on Midland lines, the edges of the cab roof had to be lowered by 3", and forty three Claughtons were recorded so altered from early in 1928. Another eleven (5905, 5912, 5915, 5917, 5926, 5933, 5940, 5942, 5968, 5976 and 5979) had their maximum height reduced in 1928-31 to pass the Caledonian 12' 11" maximum, and got a very much shorter chimney, cut-down cab roof, and dome. The whistle, hitherto vertical above the cab, changed to horizontal in front of the cab, and shorter pop safety valves were put across the centre line instead of along it.
Two oddities were noted; 5926 was fitted with one of the short chimneys whilst still in pre-1928 livery, but without any of the other alterations, but was not one of those transferred to the Mid-

2222 in March 1913 now finish painted and lined, has acquired a small cover for part of the reversing gear ahead of the splasher, and also sandshield in front of the leading coupled wheels, which were the driving wheels.

No.13's official building date was July 1920 but it was not put into traffic until March 1921 and without a name. In July 1922 it was named VINDICTIVE as here in August 1922, and then in October 1922 its number was changed to 2430 by exchanging numbers with a G2 class 0-8-0 goods engine. Note it is in unlined black but does have armorial..

land. Probably it was Crewe's guinea-pig for that type of chimney, and when it had its number moved to cab, normal chimney was fitted. 5943 got the same treatment in 1928, maybe acquiring the short chimney from 5926, and during that year, it was fitted with an experimental smoke deflector, clipped to the front of a short chimney. On both 5926 and 5943 these extra-ordinary differences were only short-lived. Despite the height reductions to permit working in Northern Division, no Claughton was ever shedded north of Carlisle.

Two Claughtons working on the Midland Division were heavily damaged in accidents, 5977 at Doe Hill on 12th February 1929, which caused it to be withdrawn in April, the first of the class to be condemned. Then on March 6th 1930, No.5971 working a passenger train from Hellifield to Carlisle, collided head-on with a ballast train at Culgaith. It was not taken out of stock until December, but not all of it was scrapped, as the bogie, coupled wheels, and frames were used in a re-construction, which combined a larger diameter boiler with three cylinders and motion, very similar to "Royal Scot" class. Derby Works gave the same treatment, at the same time, to 5902 SIR FRANK REE which retained its name, although on new curved plates instead of its straight ones. 5971's LNW CROXTETH nameplates died with the damaged portions of that engine, and the rebuilt 5971 remained without a name until October 1933, when curved plates with the CROXTETH name were fitted. Un-officially, and somewhat to the chagrin of the LMS authorities, these re-constructions became widely known as "Baby Scots", and by 1934 had totalled fifty two, the first forty two being regarded as Claughton "renewals", and retaining their names and numbers. Actually, parts from Claughtons went only into the first twelve, the others being completely new. Then in 1934, the forty two with random Claughton numbers were gathered together, in order of date of rebuilding, and were renumbered 5500 to 5541. The prototype No.5971 became 5500, and the "Croxteth" name, (only restored in October 1933) suffered a second demise in July 1934. The LNWR war memorial engine 5964 PATRIOT was withdrawn in that month, but its name and the description of the reason for it, were continued by applying it (on new curved cast plates) to 5500, and the class of 52 were then officially dubbed "Patriot" class.

Of the Claughtons to retain substantially their original appearance, the last to survive were 5951 and 5984 both withdrawn in October 1935, the former without physical alteration, but 5984 had been modified slightly to permit working to Midland loading gauge; neither ever carried a name.

(below) **1191, to traffic in May 1913, was second of the remaining nine of the order for ten. They and the following fifty built to October 1917 were fitted with two pairs of safety valves, did not have the two small windows, and brake pipe was inside the cab. Tender only had single beading, but they and the ten built in 1914, still had D frame slots. Note lamp sockets.** *LNWR Society.*

CLAUGHTON 4-CYLINDER 4-6-0 EXPRESS PASSENGER ENGINES

LNW No.	NAME	Built	LMS No.	Applied	Caprotti	Larger Boiler	With-drawn
2222	SIR GILBERT CLAUGHTON	1/13	5900	6/25	—	—	3/35
1161	SIR ROBERT TURNBULL	5/13	5901	12/25	—	—	5/33
1191	SIR FRANK REE	5/13	5902	12/26	—	—	11/30
21	DUKE OF SUTHERLAND	6/13	5903	4/27	—	—	4/33
163	HOLLAND HIBBERT	6/13	5904	7/26	—	—	12/34
650	LORD RATHMORE	6/13	5905	5/27	—	—	2/33
1159	RALPH BROCKLEBANK	7/13	5906	2/26	—	5/28	2/37
1319	SIR FREDERICK HARRISON	5/13	5907	6/26	—	—	1/33
1327	ALFRED FLETCHER	5/13	5908	8/26	8/26	12/28	9/36
2046	CHARLES N.LAWRENCE	6/13	5909	3/27	—	—	2/35
250	J.A.BRIGHT	8/14	5910	4/27	—	5/28	4/37
260	W.E.DORRINGTON	8/14	5911	5/26	—	—	3/34
1131	LORD FABER	8/14	5912	2/26	—	—	2/35
1429	COLONEL LOCKWOOD	9/14	5913	6/27	—	—	8/34
209	J.BRUCE ISMAY	9/14	5914	12/26	—	—	12/34
668	RUPERT GUINNESS	9/14	5915	6/27	—	—	11/34
856	E.TOOTAL BROADHURST	9/14	5916	6/27	—	—	12/32
1567	CHARLES J.CROPPER	10/14	5917	8/26	—	—	9/34
2239	FREDERICK BAYNES	9/14	5918	4/27	—	—	3/35
2401	LORD KITCHENER	10/14	5919	4/27	—	—	9/34
511	GEORGE MACPHERSON	7/16	5920	1/27	—	—	4/35
695	SIR ARTHUR LAWLEY	7/16	5921	1/27	—	—	11/34
968	LORD KENYON	7/16	5922	12/26	—	—	9/34
1093	GUY CALTHROP (SIR added 3/19)	7/16	5923	3/28	—	—	6/35
1345	JAMES BISHOP	8/16	5924	2/27	—	—	9/34
2174	E.C.TRENCH	8/16	5925	2/27	—	—	3/33
2204	SIR HERBERT WALKER (K.C.B. from 4/17)	8/16	5926	6/26	—	—	1/33
2221	SIR FRANCIS DENT	8/16	5927	6/26	7/28	7/28	12/36
2238	CHARLES H.DENT	8/16	5928	9/26	—	—	1/34
2395	J.A.F.ASPINALL	9/16	5929	2/27	—	—	3/35
37	G.R.JEBB	2/17	5930	3/27	—	—	10/34
154	CAPTAIN FRYATT	3/17	5931	4/26	—	—	5/34
155	I.T.WILLIAMS (SIR THOMAS WILLIAMS from 12/19)	3/17	5932	2/27	—	—	4/35
162	—	3/17	5933	6/27	—	—	12/32
186	—	3/17	5934	5/27	—	—	1/35
713	—	3/17	5935	12/26	—	—	2/33
1334	—	4/17	5936	12/26	—	—	8/32
2042	—	4/17	5937	3/27	—	—	11/34
2097	—	4/17	5938	1/27	—	—	2/35
2230	CLIO (from 7/22)	5/17	5939	3/24	—	—	6/35
1019	COLUMBUS (from 2/22)	5/17	5940	2/27	—	—	9/34
1335	—	5/17	5941	3/27	—	—	8/34
2366	—	5/17	5942	5/27	—	—	8/32
2373	TENNYSON (from 1/22)	5/17	5943	7/26	—	—	8/34
2411	—	6/17	5944	9/23	—	—	2/33
2420	INGESTRE (from 1/23)	6/17	5945	6/27	—	—	4/34
2427	DUKE OF CONNAUGHT (from 1/22)	6/17	5946	5/27	6/28	6/28	2/41
2431	—	6/17	5947	3/24	—	—	2/35
2445	BALTIC (from 3/23)	7/17	5948	3/27	6/28	6/28	4/37
2450	—	7/17	5949	4/26	—	—	8/32
116	—	7/17	5950	11/23	—	—	10/34
159	—	8/17	5951	2/27	—	—	10/35
171	—	8/17	5952	2/27	—	—	12/32
986	BUCKINGHAM (from 3/22)	8/17	5953	2/27	—	5/28	9/36
1085	—	8/17	5954	3/27	—	—	12/32
1103	—	9/17	5955	3/27	—	—	5/35
2122	—	9/17	5956	3/27	—	—	3/34
2368	—	9/17	5957	5/27	9/28	9/28	2/36
2416	—	9/17	5958	6/27	—	—	10/32
2426	—	10/17	5959	10/26	—	—	6/32
69	—	1/20	5960	6/26	—	—	3/34

499 built in May 1920 has cab rail, two pairs sandshields, and pyrometer connection, but does not have oil boxes, and would be one of the last to be fitted with Ramsbottom safety valves as original equipment. Here it is standing in Stalybridge station in 1922.

178	—	1/20	5961	11/23	—	—	10/34
194	—	1/20	5962	2/27	7/28	7/28	12/35
972	—	1/20	5963	1/27	—	—	12/32
1914	*PATRIOT In Memory of the Fallen LNWR Employees 1914-19*	1/20	5964	6/26	—	—	7/34
484	—	2/20	5965	11/26	—	—	9/34
1177	*BUNSEN (from 3/22)*	1/20	5966	2/26	—	—	10/32
1407	*L/CORPL J.A.CHRISTIE V.C. (from 2/22)*	2/20	5967	2/27	—	—	11/34
1599	*JOHN O'GROAT (from 8/22)*	2/20	5968	11/26	—	—	1/35
2179	—	1/20	5969	1/27	—	—	9/34
2499	*PATIENCE (from 8/22)*	2/20	5970	2/27	—	7/28	12/35
2511	*CROXTETH (from 7/23)*	2/20	5971	7/23	—	—	12/30
1726	—	3/20	5972	3/27	—	4/28	5/37
1741	—	3/20	5973	8/26	—	—	12/32
1747	—	3/20	5974	9/26	—	—	8/32
12	*TALISMAN (from 1/23)*	4/20	5975	1/27	6/28	6/28	5/37
2035	*PRIVATE E.SYKES V.C. (2/22-4/26)*	3/20	5976	1/27	—	—	3/35
2083	—	3/20	5977	2/27	—	—	4/29
2231	—	3/20	5978	12/26	—	—	5/34
2268	*FROBISHER (from 8/22)*	3/20	5979	3/24	—	—	4/34
85	—	4/20	5980	5/26	—	—	1/35
98	—	4/20	5981	1/27	—	—	6/34
103	—	4/20	5982	6/27	—	—	11/32
201	—	4/20	5983	6/26	—	—	10/32
499	—	5/20	5984	4/26	—	—	10/35
808	—	5/20	5985	5/27	—	—	6/32
1092	—	5/20	5986	4/26	—	4/28	11/35
1096	—	5/20	5987	1/27	—	—	8/32
1097	*PRIVATE W.WOOD V.C. (2/22-4/26)*	5/20	5988	1/27	—	—	5/35
1133	—	5/20	5989	3/26	—	—	11/34
1326	—	6/20	5990	7/27	—	—	4/35
2059	*C.J.BOWEN COOKE (from 10/20)*	5/20	5991	7/28	—	—	2/35
2090	—	6/20	5992	6/26	—	—	10/32
2095	—	6/20	5993	1/27	—	5/28	5/36
6	—	6/20	5994	6/26	—	—	6/35
8	—	6/20	5995	4/27	—	—	2/34
10	---	7/20	5996	11/23	---	---	2/33
11	---	7/20	5997	6/27	---	---	3/33

LNW No.	NAME	Built	LMS No.	Applied	Caprotti	Larger Boiler	With-drawn
2101	—	6/20	5998	12/26	—	—	8/34
2430	*VINDICTIVE (7/22- 8/36) **	7/20	5999	3/27	—	4/28	6/37
15	—	7/20	6000	2/27	—	—	3/33
23	—	8/20	6001	4/26	—	—	10/34
30	*THALABA (from 12/22)*	8/20	6002	3/27	—	—	9/34
32	—	8/20	6003	6/26	—	—	10/34
42	*PRINCESS LOUISE (2/22-6/35)***	8/20	6004	11/26	—	4/28	4/49
63	—	8/20	6005	2/27	—	—	8/32
68	—	8/20	6006	11/26	—	—	12/32
102	—	8/20	6007	12/26	—	—	10/34
110	*LADY GODIVA (from 5/23)*	9/20	6008	2/27	—	—	12/32
119	—	9/20	6009	6/27	—	—	5/34
149	—	3/21	6010	8/26	—	—	8/32
150	*ILLUSTRIOUS (from 5/23)*	3/21	6011	1/27	—	—	2/33
152	—	3/21	6012	6/26	—	—	8/32
156	—	3/21	6013	3/27	7/28	7/28	3/36
157	—	4/21	6014	1/27	—	—	9/34
158	*PRIVATE E.SYKES V.C. (from 4/26)*	4/21	6015	5/26	—	—	3/33
161	—	4/21	6016	8/27	—	—	1/35
169	*BREADALBANE (from 3/23)*	4/21	6017	11/26	—	8/28	10/40
179	*PRIVATE W.WOOD V.C. (from 4/26)*	4/21	6018	1/28	—	—	2/33
180	*LLEWELLYN (from 4/23)*	4/21	6019	4/26	—	—	12/34
183	—	5/21	6020	6/28	—	—	7/35
192	*BEVERE (from 7/23)*	5/21	6021	5/27	—	—	2/34
205	—	5/21	6022	11/26	—	—	1/33
207	*SIR CHARLES CUST (from 12/21)*	5/21	6023	6/27	8/28	8/28	7/41
208	—	5/21	6024	12/26	—	—	3/35
210	—	5/21	6025	5/27	—	—	8/35
211	—	6/21	6026	3/27	—	—	12/32
517	—	6/21	6027	9/26	—	—	1/33
1216	—	6/21	6028	4/26	—	—	9/34
1220	—	6/21	6029	1/27	5/28	5/28	12/35

** Numbered 13 from 7/20 to 10/22. ** Allotted 46004 by British Railways but never carried.*

Included to show how and where, the LNWR displayed a locomotive's shed allocation. The oval, white enamelled plate had the shed code number in black figures, and was carried in a holder fixed to the rear of the cab roof. That arrangement was continued to the end of 1930 but engines shopped in 1931-34 had the shed plate moved from the cab to the smokebox door. From January 1935 the enamelled plates were superseded by the LMS cast iron plates.

(above) **650 on 28th June 1915 leaving Carlisle with the 8.30 a.m. to Euston now has sandshields also to middle wheels, and was one of four (1159, 2046, and 2239 were the others) fitted with combined lamp iron and socket, but only 2239 kept them other than briefly. Note slight chamfering of buffer beam lower corners consequently of one of first ten fouling a platform edge at Bletchley in August 1913. All ten were given this alteration.** *LCGB Ken Nunn Collection.*

(left) **713, built in March 1917, shows the larger cut made to those after the first ten, and to which they were soon altered. It was the third of those without a name (162 and 186 preceded it) the war having caused this departure from the LNWR naming tradition.** *F.W.Goslin per The Gresley Society.*

Note buffer beam cut-out difference between 5929 and 6016 at Rugby 26th March 1932. *L.Hanson.*

1161 as here (and only 2222) were fitted from 1918 with these splash shields on the bogie to guard against throw-up by a pilot engine. Both had discarded them by 1920. *F.W.Goslin per The Gresley Society.*

1914 built in January 1920 was the first to have Ross pop safety valves, which then became standard. Here in Manchester (London Rd) it has cab rail, small cover to reversing gear, and two pairs of sand shields, but does not have the Beames oil boxes, so is entirely to Bowen Cooke's ideas.

183, built in May 1921, was the first of the final batch of ten, and shows the detail changes that Beames introduced. Sandshields were removed as more trouble than effective, the smokebox door got an extra clip (at its base), the reversing gear cover was made bigger, and at both sides, two small 3-feed oil boxes were clipped behind the boiler handrail to serve the coupled wheel axles. *A.G.Ellis.*

1599, seen at Crewe South shed, was built in February 1920 but was only named from August 1922 when it got JOHN O'GROAT. Provision had been made for a pyrometer, but was not fitted, and the outlet on the smokebox is blanked off. Although lining was resumed from late 1921, this one did not get it applied, nor did it have LNW armorial.

2366, built May 1917, has the original items of Ramsbottom safety valves, pyrometer connection still fitted, and has had two pairs sandshields and cab cross rail added, which indicates a 1920 photograph. The purpose of the indicator shelter on this occasion is not known.

2035 PRIVATE E.SYKES V.C. was named after an engineering labourer at Mossley. It was one of three engines named in February 1922 to honour LNWR employees who had won the Victoria Cross in the 1914-18 war. Working a Liverpool-Leeds express it has called at Stalybridge, and, in 1922, is still fitted with two pairs of sandshields, and carries the armorial although unlined. *Real Photos.*

2222 was the only one of the class changed to burn oil fuel during the 1921 coal strike, and had a single, large diameter tank put into the coal bunker of a 1916 type tender. The tank was removed later that year. Note that 2222 has twin Ramsbottom safety valves, to which it had been changed in 1915, and still carries two pairs of sandshields to the coupled wheels.

208 still in LNW numbering and plain black painting was one of thirty seven in this class adapted to burn oil during the May-November 1926 coal strike, and has the two cylindrical tanks usually fitted.

SIR HERBERT WALKER K.C.B. converted for oil burning in 1926. It has number plate on smokebox door but lacks number anywhere else. *LNWR Society.*

At Camden shed on 16th August 1923, un-named 32, and 42 PRINCESS LOUISE are being prepared to work the Royal Train to Carlisle taking King George V on his annual trip to Balmoral. When new in August 1920, No.32 was plain black, had pops, and a 1916 design tender. Here it is in fully lined livery with armorial, but has changed to Ramsbottom safety valves and to 1913 design tender. *Real Photos.*

1567 CHARLES J.CROPPER built in October 1914 is in the unlined black which had to be adopted after the outbreak of the 1914-18 war. Only the first twelve, those built in 1913, and No.250 with 260 built in August 1914 were originally given lining. Note there is no armorial.

2221 SIR FRANCIS DENT at Stalybridge in 1920 shows that the only relief to the black was on the buffer beam and the background to the number plate. The buffer beam did however have a rectangular panel of a thin black line, with rounded corners.

1914 PATRIOT was nominated as the Company's war memorial engine, and at first had the usual red background to its number plate. Even that was considered too garish, so was repainted black.

192 on 30th October 1921 at Irlams o' th' Height and on trial with 16-coach 494 tons load running on the L&Y line from Manchester to Blackpool. In March 1921 the LNW acquired the L&Y.

2401 LORD KITCHENER on the West Coast Main Line with the daily express meat train from Aberdeen going to London.

2450 leaving Carlisle on an up express in either 1924 or 1925 and restored to fully lined LNWR livery. It became LMS 5949 in April 1926.

207 SIR CHARLES CUST is at Kenton working from Liverpool to London. In December 1921 that name was permanently applied to 207.

No.8 which was never named has a Windermere-London express near Lancaster. It is in wartime black paint without lining and is likely to be in 1920 or 1921, because it had lining put on in 1922.

1429 COLONEL LOCKWOOD is at Kenton on this down Belfast boat train in 1923. Note this very early use of containers for passengers' luggage. *Real Photos.*

5900 fitted for burning oil fuel during the 1926 coal strike is climbing away from Oxenholme on the 10.00 a.m. Euston to Glasgow express.

5919 LORD KITCHENER is included to show the coupled wheel balance weights, because if they were visible, the coupling rods were not, being hidden by the valance, and when so placed, were disliked by photographers. 5919 is at Crewe North shed on 17th July 1932. *W.L.Good.*

5926 SIR HERBERT WALKER K.C.B. reverted to coal firing whilst it still had number on tender, and here had both chimney and cab roof cut down presumably to pass Scottish gauge. With no alteration to dome this was pointless when the latter's height remained at 13' 5½" from rail level against the 13' 0" maximum applicable in Scotland.

5940 COLUMBUS has been cut down to pass the 13' 0" maximum height of the Glasgow & South Western gauge, eleven (5905, 5912, 5915, 5917, 5926, 5933, 5940, 5942, 5968, 5976 and 5979) being altered from September 1928. Note the safety valves are set athwart.

5968 JOHN O'GROAT has shorter pop valves. These altered engines usually had tender changed to R.O.D. type as they carried 7 tons and 4000 gallons, against 6 tons and 3000 gallons in the 1916 LNW tender. That extra capacity was of help to engines working the Leeds-Glasgow trains via the Settle and Carlisle line.

(above) **5964 PATRIOT, despite being the LNWR war memorial engine, went to the Midland in September 1930. Chimney, dome, and safety valves did not need altering, but the height to the sides of the cab roof had to be reduced by 3". It was also usual to change their tender to the higher capacity R.O.D. type, but here at Stafford on 25th March 1934 it had regained the standard LNW 1916 design, and was back on the LNW.**

(right) **6005 took that number in March 1927, and had number plate put on to its smokebox door, of the usual type with wheel & handle also four clips for fastening.** *A.G.Ellis.*

(below) **5900 SIR GILBERT CLAUGHTON had this type of smokebox door fitted prior to June 1932, which depended on just eight clips for tightness. Note lower position for top lamp iron, and that it kept number plate to withdrawal as seen here awaiting cutting-up at Crewe Works 3rd March 1935.** *L.Hanson.*

5990 was also changed to a smokebox door without wheel and handle but did not have any number plate fitted on the door. The gloss on this LMS red paint certainly rivals the famed LNW 'blackberry black'.

5964 PATRIOT on 6th April 1931 at Wellingborough shed has had Midland Division shed plate 16 (Kentish Town) put on to smokebox door, as was customary on that line. *L.Hanson.*

5955 at Kentish Town shed on 12th February 1933 shows that not all this class working on the Midland had shed allocation plate fitted. *W.L.Good.*

5939 CLIO at Nothampton on 25th March 1934, has the 1916 design tender with longer frames having vertical rear edge and slots of different shape, described as 'square oval'. All the 110 engines built from July 1916 were provided with this type, and to which most of the earlier engines were changed whilst still LNWR.

5947 is at Rugby on 16th December 1933 and having needed replacement buffers, has been fitted with the Stanier design which had square instead of circular flange, and parallel instead of taper shank. Others so fitted, and all noted in 1935 were 5909, 5912, 5920, 5951 and 5994. *W.L.Good.*

5971 built as LNW 2511 in February 1920 and without a name, was named CROXTETH in June 1923, when it was the first to get LMS red painting lined single yellow, 18" numerals on tender, 4½ inch LMS on cab side, and cast number plate on its smokebox door.

5900 SIR GILBERT CLAUGHTON in June 1925 has red livery with the 14" circular armorial on cab. That replaced the small LMS from mid-December 1923 officially, but it was well into 1924 before Crewe used it. For its Darlington Centenary appearance it got vertical lining as an extra on its tender. Compare with 5971 and 5947 above, which have the standard tender lining.

5951 on 4th August 1935 has arrived at Llandudno Junction from London on *THE WELSHMAN* and has cast plate 6A for Chester. From January 1935 the LMS introduced an "all-line" allocation list. 5951 was lucky to get one of these plates - it was withdrawn in the following October .

5943 TENNYSON had this experimental smoke deflector fitted at the front of its chimney in 1928, and Royal Scot No.6131 was similarly fitted at the same time, but both proved only short-lived. Note that 5943 has one of the 1913/14 tenders with D slots in the frames.

5965 here in 1932 with red livery had smokebox plate fitted when changed from LNW 484 in November 1926, but has had it removed, although the fixing bolts remain visible. LNW shed plate 8 shows it was allocated to Rugby.

6009 at Kentish Town on 18th May 1932, with cab roof altered to pass Midland gauge, shows the single yellow lining was applied to R.O.D. type tender. Its rear panel carries both an oval G.C. and a square LMS type tender number plate, but their numbers cannot be deciphered.

5904 HOLLAND HIBBERT at Elmsthorpe is on a semi-fast from Nuneaton to Leicester Midland (London Road) station. The normal LNW style curved edge to the cab roof is clearly seen.

(below) **5931 CAPTAIN FRYATT still in black and without lining is about to work an express on the West Coast main line, to Euston from Crewe. It was rare indeed for a Claughton to be a pilot engine, the train engine here being 5630 JOHN RUSKIN.**

5944 still in 1923 painting is leaving Oxenholme on an Edinburgh to Manchester train although the headlamp code is misleading for a passenger train.

5955 working a cattle train on the Midland main line at Elstree. The changed shape of cab roof edge is clear to see, and even with an R.O.D. tender having one ton more coal capacity, this crew are definitely of the "belt and braces" mentality.

5958 at Oxenholme is hauling this Royal Scot to Crewe for repair and that was where the Claughton was shedded. *Lens of Sutton.*

5940 COLUMBUS on 6th June 1933 is at Bletchley on an up local from Crewe. In 1928 its heights were reduced so as to be able to work north of Carlisle but none of those so altered were ever shedded in Scotland. *L.Hanson.*

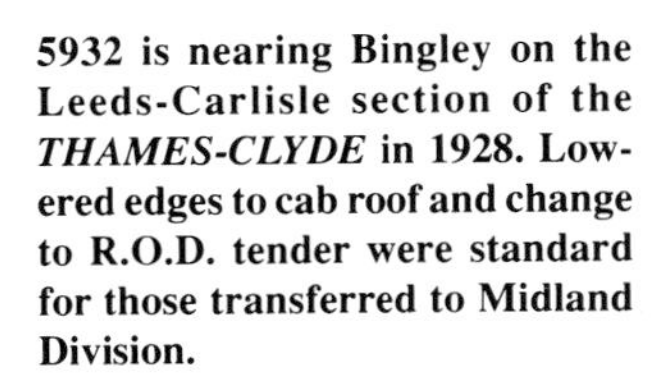

5932 is nearing Bingley on the Leeds-Carlisle section of the *THAMES-CLYDE* in 1928. Lowered edges to cab roof and change to R.O.D. tender were standard for those transferred to Midland Division.

5960 with an express parcels train is leaving Oxenholme for the north in the summer of 1926 after it had been fitted in June for burning oil fuel.

5963 piloting 9527 on this goods train in 1930 is at Berkhamsted; about as unlikely a combination as could be imagined. *A.G.Ellis.*

5990 has arrived in Euston on 10th October 1929 with an express and still had normal smokebox door at that date. *R.Blencowe Collection.*

(above) **6001 at Derby station is about to depart with an express for St Pancras. Its Midland 16 shedplate shows that its allocation was Kentish Town.** *T.G.Hepburn.*

5908 ALFRED FLETCHER in August 1926 was the first major attempt by Beames to improve the breed. Retaining the original boiler design, except for Ross instead of Ramsbottom safety valves (which was effective from 1920) he superseded the Walschaerts valve gear and piston valves by Caprotti poppet valves. The locomotive also then acquired the red livery. 5908 (seen here on a heavy express goods) was given an extensive series of indicator tests. The poppet valves together with alteration to piston rings, gave a reduced coal consumption of about 20%. No others were altered like 5908, but nine more got Caprotti gear along with a larger boiler. *W.L.Good.*

5912 from 1928 worked mainly on the Midland between St Pancras and Leeds and here is on shed at Nottingham. In early 1932 it got this taller chimney and Kylchap blastpipe from 6001, which it is then thought to have kept until its February 1935 withdrawal. *T.G.Hepburn.*

6001 had its cab roof edges altered in April 1928, and the higher capacity R.O.D. tender coupled, so that it could work on the Midland main line, but at that stage, it retained standard LNWR chimney.

5953 BUCKINGHAM, reversing out of Crewe station, shows how the first ten rebuildsappeared when reboilered in 1928, this one in May.

5953 still had Cooke buffers when its first smoke deflectors were put on, and they were simply flat sided sheets.

5906 RALPH BROCKLEBANK changed in May to this six inch larger diameter boiler, working at 200 instead of 175 p.s.i. It was one of a batch of ten so rebuilt in April-June 1928. The smoke deflectors were a later addition, as seen at Crewe North on 22nd July 1934. ***W.L.Good.***

5910 J.A.BRIGHT also changed to the 5' 5" boiler in May 1928 and here has had deflectors added, and has been changed also to Stanier buffers. Its LNW shedplate shows it allocated to Preston so is a 1933 or 1934 photograph.

5972 here has acquired the later type deflectors, the first type not proving sufficiently effective. The Beames oil boxes were retained; they were now mounted on the boiler cladding. Note change to Stanier type buffers by 2nd June 1935 where it is caught by the camera at Bournville shed. The shed plate reads 12B, Carlisle Upperby.

6004 had its name removed in June 1935 to avoid duplication by that name being put on to 4-6-2 No.6204. Here with deflectors and Stanier buffers it is at Rugby shed on March 23rd 1947 having considerably outlived the other nine of this type. Eight were withdrawn between November 1935 and June 1937, and the other one in November 1940, but 6004 survived to April 1949. It was allocated British Railways number 46004, but that was never applied.
C.F.H.Oldham.

6017 BREADALBANE at Crewe North as reboilered in April 1928 shows the livery particularly well, even the 5X power class on the cab. The height to the edge of the cab roof was reduced to suit the Midland line load gauge. 6017 duly acquired smoke deflectors and Stanier buffers.

5986 as reboilered in April 1928 shows the additional handrail put on the rear half of the smokebox side, and also the red painting with yellow lining, which was standard livery for the rebuilds.

5970 ex works 15th May 1928 was the last of the ten of this type. Here a direct "before & after", comparison can be made, 5930 being as built. The pair are about to leave Crewe for London, on 26th May 1928, with the 8.30 a.m. ex-Carlisle. Only eleven days ex-works, 5970 only worked to Rugby. *C.A.J.Nevett.*

5975 TALISMAN is as rebuilt in June 1928, and there is no doubt about it having pyrometer connection, which appears to have been a standard fitting on the 5' 5" diameter boilers. *Real Photos.*

6013 was rebuilt to larger boiler and Caprotti valve gear in August 1928, but was still in that condition when seen here on 23rd April 1928 near Wembley working the 11.40 a.m. Manchester to Euston. No doubt smoke deflectors would be added at its next works visit. *LCGB Ken Nunn Collection.*

5908 ALFRED FLETCHER had been fitted with Caprotti valve gear as early as August 1926, and then in December 1928 received the last of the twenty large diameter boilers. Here in 1932, flat sided smoke deflectors have been added, of the type which did not prove sufficiently effective. Its LNW 26 (Edge Hill) plate shows it returning to Liverpool, and climbing Camden bank on an express.

5975 TALISMAN seen here in 1936 at Hest Bank station has the more effective deflectors resulting from the inward inclination of the top portion. In addition to the larger boiler and Caprotti valve gear which it got in 1928, this view shows the larger diameter chimney put on in 1932 in conjunction with a Kyala blastpipe, aimed at softening the blast. 5975 was the only one so fitted. *Locofotos.*

5958 was so numbered in June 1927 when smokebox plate was fitted, and here it would be ex-works from its next general repair, with fully lined red painting. Asd then applied, the 14" figures and letters did not have any counter-shading.

5911 W.E.DORRINGTON here ex-works at Crewe South on 9th March 1929 has the fully lined red painting with matching 14" serif letters and numbers showing the 1928 standard style in prime condition. This made amends for it being the subject of rough treatment in May 1926 when being renumbered by loss of its plates, and only getting 5911 in tiny figures.

6015 carries the S on its cab denoting Special Limit working, and here has the name PRIVATE E.SYKES V.C. transferred to it in April 1926, when it was another to suffer the loss of LNW plates, but along with the name it *was* accorded a smokebox numberplate. *Railway Photos.*

5941 has the 12 noon ex-Euston at Whitmore troughs on 7th June 1930 when it had already lost the smokebox plate fitted to it in March 1927. Continuity of coach roof line was not a strong feature on the West Coast main line trains.

This is a Liverpool-London express on Whitmore troughs, probably in 1930 and shows a direct comparison of two Claughtons. Leading engine 5961 is still to the LNW load gauge but the named train engine is one of those with heights from rail reduced to pass the much more rstricted Northern Division gauge. The chimney and dome emphasize the difference, as do the safety valves placed across instead of along the centtre line.

(above) **5916 E.TOOTAL BROADHURST piloting 'Scot' 6142 is at Camden on 16th July 1932 with this northbound express. The Claughtons transferred to the Midland Division did not take all the purchased R.O.D. tenders with them, and 5916 never had its cab roof edges altered to Midland gauge as it was withdrawn in December 1932, only five months after being seen here.**

It is well that the photographer put 5926 on his print to help identification here, because, simply doing a bit of shunting at Crewe on 12th June 1926, SIR HERBERT WALKER K.C.B. has just lost its 2204 brass plates for the miserly 6" painted figures, at the works visit when it was also fitted for oil burning.

6002 THALABA is leaving Chester with this express for Llandudno on 13th August 1932. Note it has been fitted with an extra clip (making five) at the base of the smokebox door.

6029 in May 1928 was the first to get larger boiler and Caprotti valves. Here in Crewe Works on 17th July 1932, the Camden based engine has been fitted with the flat sided deflectors. *W.L.Good.*

5946 on shed at Crewe North; and from this angle the holder on cab roof rear edge for the LNW shedplate can be seen. It also shows sanding has been changed from gravity to steam applied.

5923 SIR GUY CALTHROP at Carlisle had changed to that number in March 1928 when it was put on cab, although only in ten inch figures, but it would be one of the last to get a smokebox number plate fitted. The engine does not have any lining, in contrast to the tender which has a prominent panel of it.

6004, fitted with large boiler from April 1928, is working this Class A goods after being fitted with LMS cast shed plate, introduced in January 1935, and is also minus its nameplates which were removed in June 1935.

5910 J.A.BRIGHT was rebuilt with large boiler in May 1928 and was able to pass at least Midland gauge. Here in c1931 it is on a local at Annan. Its shedplate reads 27 denoting Preston.

5929 J.A.F.ASPINALL was withdrawn in the month after 5947, which is the engine behind it, and 5929 retained Cooke buffers through to withdrawal. The engine is marked CONDEMNED but its tender has been taken away for further use.

Finally - a Claughton photograph about which I hope that you can add to my knowledge. 5997 was at Upperby shed on 14th April 1930 seen carrying this wicker hamper in front of its smokebox. What is likely to have been in the basket, and where would the Claughton be taking it?

My guess is that the contents would be the shed's used cleaning cloths, towels from the mess-room, or the enginemen's barracks. The extra man on the footplate could well be in charge of the basket and contents, and in process of transporting them to a laundry adjacent to Citadel station, from which 5997 would be going to attach to a train.

PATRIOTS - The end of the Claughtons?

45500 of British Railways had been 5500 on the LMS since 1934 and prior to that was 5971 from July 1923, when it was changed from the LNW number 2511 which that Claughton had been given when it was built in February 1920.

The PATRIOT name, with its supplementary 'In memory of the fallen LNWR employees 1914 - 1919' was first used for the Claughton specially numbered 1914 and built in January 1920, when it was fitted with rectangular plates akin to Crewe style. That engine was renumbered 5964 from June 1926, until its withdrawal in June 1934, when those nameplates became museum items.

Claughton 5971 named CROXTETH was scrapped following the considerable damage that it sustained in a collision at Culgaith, between Carlisle and Appleby, on 6th March 1930, but its main frame, and large-boss coupled wheel centres were salvaged for further use.

The 5971 number re-appeared in November 1930, but without the 'Croxteth' name which was not restored until October 1933. In the 1934 re-numbering 5971 changed to 5500, which kept the 'Croxteth' name until that was changed to 'Patriot' from 25th February 1937. As such, it and the supplementary wording, were on curved cast plates, as seen in the photograph below.

5971 and the other re-constructed Claughton's done in 1930, had the 5' 5" boiler as put on twenty of the original Claughtons in 1928, combined with 1927 Royal Scot engine arrangement, but incorporating the radial bogie, and large-boss coupled wheels of a Claughton. In the two 1930 replacements 5971 and 5902 (5501 from 1934) the only original Claughton items were modified frame, coupled wheel centres, radial bogie, and whistle. In addition to their change of number, both also had change of name, 5501 subsequently changing from SIR FRANK REE to ST DUNSTANS. Thus it was not until the demise of 45500 on 11th March 1961, and that of 45502 on 26th August 1961 that the final Claughton evidence was extinguished.

Those which became 5502 to 5511 had radial bogie truck of the Claughton design, and their whistle type. The others owed nothing to Claughtons except the whistle, retention of LNW bestowed name, and the LMS number which was allocated to them in 1923.

First LMS No.	Date Rebuilt	Where Rebuilt	1934 Renumbering
5971	11/30	Derby	5500
5902	12/30	— " —	5501
5959	7/32	Crewe	5502
5985	7/32	— " —	5503
5987	8/32	— " —	5504
5949	8/32	— " —	5505
5974	8/32	— " —	5506
5936	8/32	— " —	5507
6010	8/32	— " —	5508
6005	9/32	— " —	5509
6012	9/32	— " —	5510
5942	9/32	— " —	5511
5966	10/32	— " —	5512
5958	10/32	— " —	5513
5983	10/32	— " —	5514
5992	10/32	— " —	5515
5982	11/32	— " —	5516
5952	2/33	— " —	5517
6006	2/33	— " —	5518
6008	2/33	— " —	5519
5954	2/33	Derby	5520
5933	3/33	— " —	5521
5973	3/33	— " —	5522
6026	3/33	Crewe	5523
5907	3/33	— " —	5524
5916	3/33	Derby	5525
5963	3/33	— " —	5526
5944	4/33	— " —	5527
5996	4/33	— " —	5528
5926	4/33	Crewe	5529
6022	4/33	— " —	5530
6027	4/33	— " —	5531
6011	4/33	— " —	5532
5905	4/33	Derby	5533
5935	5/33	— " —	5534
5997	5/33	— " —	5535
6018	5/33	Crewe	5536
6015	8/33	— " —	5537
6000	8/33	— " —	5538
5925	8/33	— " —	5539
5901	8/33	— " —	5540
5903	9/33	— " —	5541

(below) **45500 PATRIOT the original Claughton rebuild, seen at Crewe North shed 16th August 1953. The rebuilt engine cost £6,266 including tender. During its 30 year life it covered 1,239,904 miles and was broken up at Crewe on 30th March 1961.** *E.V.Fry*